TREPANG
CHINA & THE STORY OF MACASSAN – ABORIGINAL TRADE

海参——

华人、望加锡人、澳洲土著人的故事

Cover
Zhou Xiaoping
Trading (detail)
2010
installation scales, trepangs
250 x 1500cm

封面
周小平
交易(细部)
2010年
材料：秤，海参
250 x 1500cm

PUBLISHED BY
CENTRE FOR CULTURAL
MATERIALS CONSERVATION
THE UNIVERSITY OF MELBOURNE
© 2011 CENTRE FOR CULTURAL
MATERIALS CONSERVATION
THE UNIVERSITY OF MELBOURNE
© IN THE INDIVIDUAL ESSAYS IS RETAINED
BY THE AUTHORS. ALL RIGHTS RESERVED.

THIS WORK IS COPYRIGHT.
APART FROM ANY USE AS PERMITTED
UNDER THE COPYRIGHT ACT 1968,
NO PART MAY BE REPRODUCED
BY ANY PROCESS WITHOUT PRIOR
WRITTEN PERMISSION.

WORKS BY JOHN BULUNBULUN:
© JOHN BULUNBULUN
LICENSED BY VISCOPY, 2011

WORK BY LAPULUNG DHAMARRANDJI:
© LAPULUNG DHAMARRANDJI
LICENSED BY VISCOPY, 2011

WORKS BY ZHOU XIAOPING:
© ZHOU XIAOPING
LICENSED BY VISCOPY, 2011

COLLABORATIVE WORKS:
© JOHN BULUNBULUN & ZHOU XIAOPING
LICENSED BY VISCOPY, 2011
NATIONAL LIBRARY OF AUSTRALIA
CATALOGUING-IN-PUBLICATION ENTRY

LANGTON, MARCIA, 1951-

TREPANG : CHINA AND THE STORY
OF MACASSAN—ABORIGINAL TRADE
/MARCIA LANGTON; EDITORS, ALEJANDRA
DUSCHATZKY, STEPHANIE HOLT.

ISBN: 9780646532165 (HBK.)

ABORIGINAL AUSTRALIANS--
COMMERCE--CHINA--HISTORY.
ABORIGINAL AUSTRALIANS--
COMMERCE--INDONESIA--HISTORY.
ART, ABORIGINAL AUSTRALIAN--
ECONOMIC ASPECTS.
CHINESE--COMMERCE--
AUSTRALIA--HISTORY.
ART, CHINESE--ECONOMIC ASPECTS.
MAKASAR (INDONESIAN PEOPLE)--
COMMERCE--AUSTRALIA--HISTORY.
CULTURAL PROPERTY--AUSTRALIA.

CORN, AARON DAVID SAMUEL.
DUSCHATSKY, ALEJANDRA.
GARAWIRRTJA, DJANGIRRAWUY.
HOLT, STEPHANIE.
MARETT, ALLAN.
UNIVERSITY OF MELBOURNE.
CENTRE FOR CULTURAL
MATERIAL CONSERVATION.

994.0049915

DESIGNED & TYPESET
BY STUDIO ROUND

PRODUCTION MANAGEMENT
BY REUBEN FOX

PRINTED IN CHINA
BY EVERBEST PRINTING CO

EXHIBITION DESIGN
BY STUDIO 505

CONTENTS
目录

FOREWORD 4
致辞

FOREWORD 6
致辞

TREPANG 14
BY MARCIA LANGTON
海参
作者：玛西亚·兰顿
TRADE IN THE 'SOUTH SEAS' 18
"南海"贸易
THE MACASSAN IN NORTH AUSTRALIA 28
澳大利亚北部的望加锡人
THE BRITISH IN NORTH AUSTRALIA 30
澳大利亚北部的英国人
SOME ABORIGINAL–MACASSAN ENCOUNTERS 36
土著与望加锡人的一些冲突
DAENG SARRO 38
邓·撒落
THE MACASSAN LEGACY AFTER THE END OF THE TRADE 40
贸易终结后的望加锡传奇
THE RESONANCE OF THE MACASSANS AND THE TREPANG TRADE 48
IN ABORIGINAL CULTURAL TRADITIONS TODAY
望加锡人和海参贸易在当今土著文化传统里的共鸣
REVIVING THE MACASSAN SPIRIT 60
望加锡精神的复苏
COMMEMORATING THE MACASSANS 64
纪念望加锡人
TREPANG: THE EXHIBITION 66
海参：展览

TO PROCLAIM THEY STILL EXIST: THE CONTEMPORARY YOLŊU 72
PERFORMANCE OF HISTORICAL MACASSAN CONTACT
BY AARON CORN AND ALLAN MARETT WITH DJAṈGIRRAWUY GARAWIRRTJA
宣告他们仍然存在：雍古族与望加锡历史性交流的当代延续
作者：艾伦·科恩(Aaron Corn)和阿伦·马瑞特(Allan Marett)及当吉拉武伊·
嘎啦维塔(Djaṉgirrawuy Garawirrtja)

CONTEMPORARY WORKS 90
当代作品

BIOGRAPHIES 137
人物简介

ACKNOWLEDGEMENTS 140
鸣谢

致辞

举办"中国澳大利亚文化年"以及此后即将举办的"澳大利亚中国文化年",为两国打造出精彩的文化交流平台。在此,我很荣幸向大家介绍这段辉煌的历史以及此次突破性展览,这次展览展出的是澳中贸易关系中首次见诸于文字记载的内容。

本次展览《海参——华人、望加锡人、澳洲土著人的故事》基于历史、艺术、社会证据,展示了18世纪初至20世纪初,澳大利亚土著人与亚洲民众之间在海参方面的贸易联系。

本次展览汇集世界各地私人珍藏品与公共机构及澳大利亚最顶级收藏机构的珍品,展出文献、制品、图画、地图、图片内容丰富,再次呈现这段交流历史,体现出华人、望加锡人、澳大利亚土著文化之间的贸易发展历程。

此外,本次展览也鲜明展示了德高望重的土著艺术家约翰·布龙·布龙与受中国古典艺术熏陶的华人艺术家周小平之间的当代艺术协作成果。

《海参》是北京首都博物馆首次举办的澳大利亚土著艺术展览。

《海参》为我们提供了探索和丰富澳中两国关系的机遇,让我们一同了解十八世纪中后期海参商人穿越中澳海洋阻隔的交流历史,让21世纪的中国人民也能了解这段历史,这是一次重温历史并确证两国密切联系的举措。

Craig Em—

国会议员Craig Emerson博士阁下
澳大利亚贸易部长

FOREWORD

The 'Year of Australian Culture in China' program and the corollary 'Year of Chinese Culture in Australia' provide a wonderful forum for cultural exchange. It is, then, a great pleasure to introduce both a remarkable story and a ground-breaking exhibition documenting the first recorded trade between Australia and China.

The exhibition, *Trepang: The Chinese & Macassan trade with Aboriginal Australia*, is founded on the historical, artistic and social evidence of Aboriginal and Asian contact around trade in trepang – or sea cucumber – from the early 18th Century to the early 20th Century.

Sourced from public collections across the globe, and from Australia's finest collecting institutions, this exhibition presents an extensive array of documents, artefacts, paintings, maps and images tracing this historical exchange and reflecting on the development of trade between the Chinese, Macassan and Aboriginal cultures.

It also presents a striking, contemporary artistic collaboration between respected Indigenous artist John Bulunbulun and classically-trained Chinese artist Zhou Xiaoping.

Trepang is the first exhibition of Indigenous Australian art to be presented at the Capital Museum of Beijing.

Trepang offers opportunities to explore and enrich the relationships between Australia and China through an understanding of the historical links that trepang traders formed as they plied the seas between the two countries from the mid- to late-1700s. To share this in the 21st Century with the people of China is an act of historical re-connection and an affirmation of our close ties.

Craig Em

The Hon Dr Craig Emerson MP
Australian Minister for Trade

致辞

　　这是一个出人意料之外的展览。它提供给中国观众（包括我自己）一个过去并不知晓的信息：中国人早在18世纪便因小小的海参与远隔重洋的澳大利亚建立起密切的往来关系。这一信息的背后还有更多的有关中国的信息，它们足以改变我们的传统认识，即中国在全球化的进程中，有相当长的一段时间是置身其外的。我们的先辈其实并没错过欧洲地理大发现之后的环球贸易大潮，一度还是广泛的国际贸易的弄潮儿。只要看看海参这种在今天国际贸易中所占比重微不足道的商品，就把中国同遥远的澳大利亚密切联系在一起，就足有说明这一点了。更不用说直到19世纪中叶笑傲世界的瓷器、丝绸和茶叶这些大宗消费品的出口贸易了。看来，德国学者弗兰克在《白银时代》中估量19世纪以前的中国在世界经济中坐头把交椅的说法似乎不虚。我想这是此次在首博的《海参》展的一个意义。

　　如果说中国在18世纪便因海参贸易与澳大利亚建立的经常联系，那么今天中国与澳大利亚之间的广泛交流就是200多年前海参贸易的继续。了解中国与澳大利亚之间绵延已久的交往，增进两国人民之间的了解，加强两国人民之间的友谊，这应该是此次展览的又一个意义。实际上，参与展览的华裔艺术家周小平先生的创作，以及以约翰·布龙·布龙先生为代表的当今澳洲艺术家的作品本身，已经证明了这种紧密交往与友谊的存在。

　　我衷心地希望以《海参》展为契机，开创中澳两国博物馆界和文化艺术界相互交流的新篇章。

郭小凌
中国首都博物馆 馆长

FOREWORD

This is a surprising exhibition. It will provide the Chinese audience (including myself) with previously unknown information. Through the tiny trepang, Chinese people had already established a close relationship with faraway Australia. Behind this information one may discover even more about China; it is enough to change our traditional understanding that has prevailed for a very long time - China's spectator role in the path to globalization. In reality our ancestors did not miss the global trade wave that followed the age of European exploration, China was actually at the forefront of expanding international trade. One only has to look at the trepang, a product that makes up a negligible portion of international trade, to see the link that closely connects China to distant Australia. Not to mention the export of porcelain, silk and tea, these mass consumer products that dominated the world in the mid 19th century. It looks like German scholar Frank's prediction in The Silver Age that before the19th century China sat on the throne of international trade is indeed the case. I believe this is one of the significances of this Trepang exhibition at the Capital Museum.

If we say China established frequent connections with Australia in the 18th century due to the trepang, then the extensive communications today between China and Australia are a continuation of the 200-year-old trepang trade. Understanding the long relationship between China and Australia will further people's understanding in both countries. This is another significant feature of the exhibition. In reality, the works of Chinese artist Mr Zhou Xiaoping, and Australian contemporary artist Mr John Bulunbulun, have already demonstrated the existence of this close relationship and friendship.

It is my sincere hope that the Trepang exhibition can be an opportunity for a new chapter in the mutual dialogue between museums and the arts community in China and Australia.

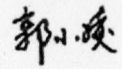

Guo Xiaoling
Director
Capital Museum, China

Paul Foelsche
Trepang Fishery Station,
Port Essington,
26 March 1875
Image courtesy of the State Library of South Australia
B10836

A large gathering of Macassan trepangers and Iwaidja assemble before the established trepang processing station. The Macassarese and Buginese fishermen, who had been trading with the resident Iwaidja clan for several centuries, knew the site as Pearl Bay and presumably supplied the settler's trepang processing plant built on the beach. A palisade and Aboriginal camp occupy the foreground and smoke can be seen billowing from the trepang factory.
Timothy Smith,
The Policeman's Eye: The Photography of Paul Foelsche, PhD thesis, University of Melbourne

Paul Foelsche
海参捕捞站,
埃辛顿港,
1875年3月26日
图片承蒙南澳州立图书馆提供
B10836

　　许多望加锡海参渔民和伊维德加族人聚在建立已久的海参加工站前面。几个世纪以来,望加锡和普吉斯渔民一直都与伊维德加族人有贸易往来,并将该地称为珍珠湾。据推测,他们向殖民者在海滩上建造的海参加工厂供应了原料。前景是一个木栅栏和土著营地,可以看见海参加工厂升起的滚滚浓烟。
Timothy Smith,
警察的眼睛:
Paul Foelsche摄影作品,博士论文
墨尔本大学

9

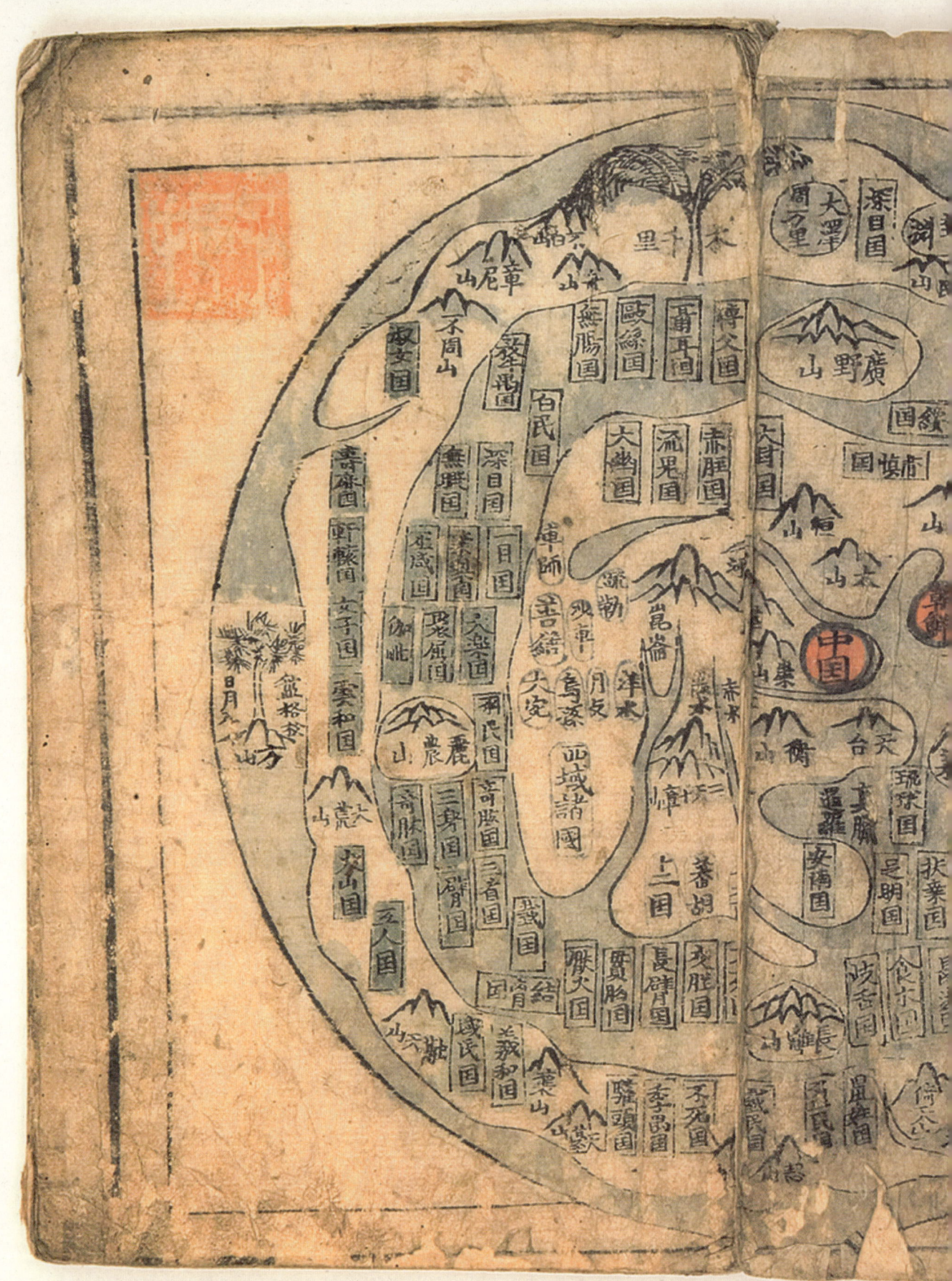

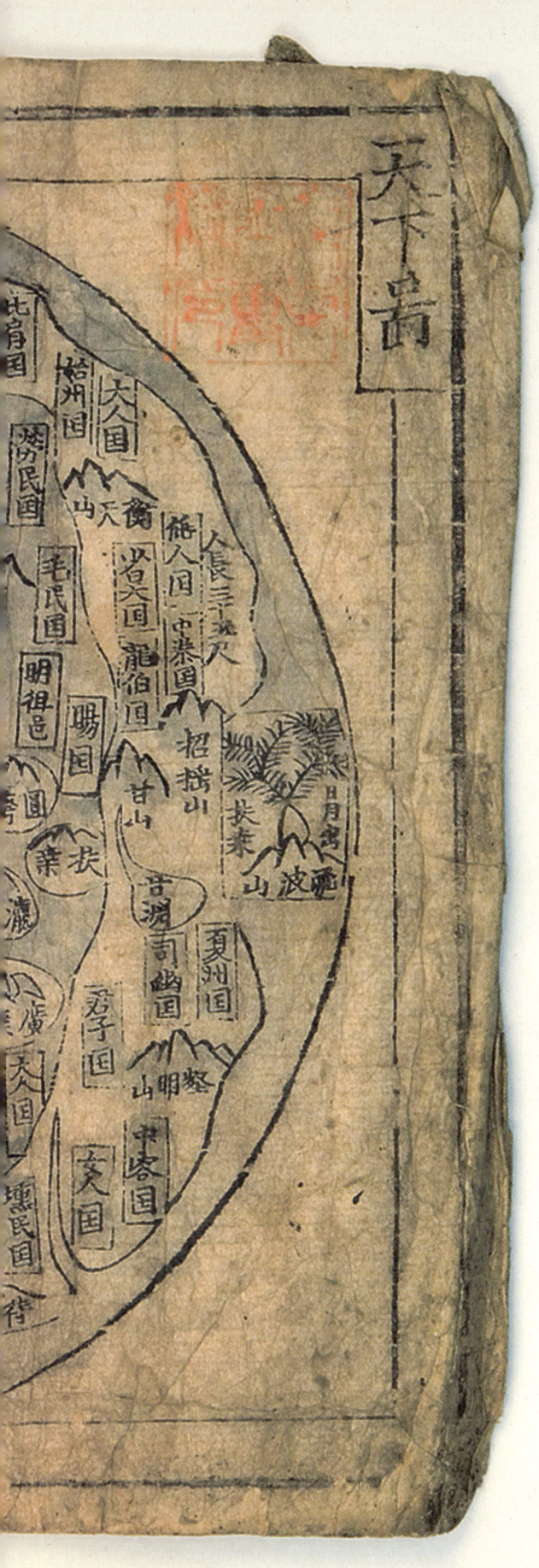

Tian Xia (World Map)
from Book 5
This atlas is thought to have been produced in the Ming Dynasty. The reverse side of the maps has large, highly stylised, and beautiful Chinese calligraphy. The maps inside this Korean book are each 29 cm x 33.5 cm and unfold to form one long continuous page. From the Dr. Hendon M. Harris, Jr. Map Collection by permission of Charlotte Harris Rees, author Secret Maps of the Ancient World www.harrismaps.com

第五册之天下（世界地图）据认为，这本地图集是在明朝绘制的。地图背面有非常别隽秀的中国书法。这本韩文书中的地图每张尺寸为29 x 33.5cm，打开后展成一张连绵不断的长幅地图。此图来自于小Hendon M. Harris博士的地图收藏，并征得《古代世界秘图》作者Charlotte Harris Rees许可。www.harrismaps.com

Da Qing yi tong tian xia quan tu [map] / Zhu Xiling hui.
This map, showing the territory of the Qing Dynasty, was made by Zhu Xiling in 1818. The Great Wall, Lop Nur Desert, the provincial divisions, capitals, cities and towns, military outposts, and main waterways and rivers are all clearly delineated. America and other Western countries are represented as an array of vague and inconsequential islands along the border of the main landmass.
Courtesy of the Hong Kong University of Science and Technology

大清一统天下全图【地图】/朱熙陵（译音）绘

此地图由朱熙陵与1818年绘制，展现出清朝的领域。长城、罗布泊沙漠、省界、首府、城镇、军事前哨、主要水道与河流 — 全都一一清楚描绘。美国和其他西方国家则被绘制为主要大陆边界沿线的一连串模糊不清、不合逻辑的岛屿。香港科技大学提供。

大清一統天下全圖

海参

作者：玛西亚·兰顿(Marcia Langton)[1]

简介

它成为梦想的主题。
约翰·考特(John Cawte)[2]

本次展览的举办，建立在两位艺术家的友谊之上。他们都是古典传统的传承人。中国合肥的周小平，曾在安徽教育学院进修古典视觉艺术；以及被高度赞誉为伊瑞佳部落分支的(Yirritja moiety)歌曲及仪式传承人、古兰巴库兰巴部落(Gurrambakurramba clan)长老约翰·布龙·布龙(John Bulunbulun)，在澳大利亚北领地阿纳姆丛林（Arnhem Land） 东中部研修古典视觉艺术。自1988年以来，经过多年的合作，他们在二百多年前先辈们跨越中国与澳大利亚北海岸之间文化、海洋、岛屿的重重阻隔、互通往来的历史事件上达成了共识。

至少从1780年起[3]，西里伯斯岛(Celebes)的海参捕捞者就抵达澳大利亚北海岸，捕捞被中国人视为美餐和壮阳药(尤其是海参汤)的海参。海参(trepang)一词源自望加锡(Makassar)语 *teripang*，通常是指海黄瓜的可食品种，如糙海参 *(Holothuria scabra)*[4]。这些远航渔民坐着小船(或称为敞舱船*perahu*)，开辟出中国与东南亚之间一条鲜为人知的贸易航线。他们主要是来自戈瓦王国(Kingdom of Gowa)(也就是现在的印度尼西亚苏拉威西岛南部)的望加锡人[5]，穿越重洋来到澳大利亚北部，在一些海湾里捕捞珍贵的海参。望加锡人有时可能是通过中国的中间人，将海参(或称海黄瓜)销售到中国港口[6]。

时至今日，澳大利亚北领地的一些土著部落仍然在重演着这些历史事件。本次展览中，周小平、约翰·布龙·布龙和其他过去及当代艺术家，一同来演示这段漫长的历史长河，并且了解当今的土著文化。这样一种纯粹的海洋动物，如何会在遥远如斯的中国人、西里伯斯岛望加锡人以及北领地土著人的历史中产生共鸣？这段故事曾出现在书籍、记录、文件、油画、绘画、物品和土著传统之中，每个故事都展示了一个多世纪以来这些主角们的勇敢、激动、财富、冲突和友谊。而故事的主旨，则是在贸易交往之中建立的友谊和联盟。本次展览的艺术品将展示这些关系及其所带来的文化财富如何延续至今。

TREPANG

By Marcia Langton[1]

INTRODUCTION

It became the subject of a dream.
John Cawte[2]

This exhibition is founded on the friendship of two artists, each inheritors of ancient traditions: Zhou Xiaoping from Hefei, classically trained in the visual art traditions at the Anhui College in China; and John Bulunbulun, a senior member of the Gurrambakurramba clan, highly regarded as a song and ceremony man of the Yirritja moiety, traditionally trained in the visual art traditions of east central Arnhem Land in the Northern Territory of Australia. After years of collaboration, dating back to 1988, they bring together their understanding of historical events that entangled their ancestors across cultures and the seas and archipelagos between China and the northern coast of Australia more than two centuries ago.

From perhaps at least 1780,[3] trepangers from Celebes were visiting the north coast of Australia to obtain trepang which Chinese people used as a delicacy and aphrodisiac, especially in soup. The term trepang derives from the Makassar word *teripang*, generally referring to the edible varieties of sea cucumber, such as *Holothuria scabra*.[4] A lesser known trade route between China and South-East Asia was plied by these seafarers in their small craft, or *perahu*. They were mostly Macassans[5] from the Kingdom of Gowa (now in southern Sulawesi, Indonesia) and they sailed to north Australia to harvest the precious trepang from some of the coastal bays of the region. The Macassans traded the trepang —or sea cucumbers—, perhaps sometimes through intermediary Chinese traders, to the ports of China.[6]

The historical resonance of these events lives on among some Aboriginal groups of the Northern Territory, Australia. In this exhibition, Zhou Xiaoping, John Bulunbulun and other artists, both historical and contemporary, have illustrated the long reach of this history into present day Aboriginal culture. How could a mere sea animal resonate in the histories of peoples as far flung as the Chinese, the Macassans of the Celebes and Aborigines of north Australia? The story has emerged from books, records, documents, paintings, drawings, objects and Aboriginal traditions, each revealing something of the bravery, excitement, wealth, conflict and friendship experienced by the protagonists for more than a century. What lies at the heart of this story is friendship and alliances forged through trade. The artworks in this exhibition show how these relationships and the cultural riches that ensued are still celebrated today.

John Bulunbulun
& Zhou Xiaoping
Discovery of trading
2009
Acrylic, ochre on canvas
231.7 x 168.3cm

约翰·布龙·布龙与周小平
发现与交易
2009年
丙烯，天然色素，布面绘画
231.7 x 168.3cm

Xiamen ji lin jin di qu di tu [map]. Manuscript map of Amoy and the surrounding region. An important early 19th century manuscript map of the port of Xiamen and the surrounding regions. The map includes the islands and settlements on Xiamen and Jinmen as well as the coastal city of Quanzhou. It shows all the principal fortifications, settlements, anchorages, and sea routes. This map provides a rarely detailed picture of this region through the eyes of an anonymous official early 19th century Chinese mapmaker, c.1810. Courtesy of the Hong Kong University of Science and Technology.

厦门及邻近地区地图【地图】。厦门港与邻近地区手绘地图。此为十九世纪初厦门港和邻近地区的重要手绘地图，包括厦门和金门的岛屿和定居点以及沿海城市泉州。

该地图绘出了所有主要要塞、定居点、停泊地点以及航海路线。

地图透过十九世纪初的一位不知姓名的中国官方制图师的眼睛，非常罕有地绘制出该地区的细部。

香港科技大学提供。

"南海"贸易

清朝统治时期（1644年至1911年）的中国，是东亚和东南亚的超级帝国。中国漫长的贸易和商业历史要追溯到宋朝（960年至1279年），中国人熟悉东印度群岛的贸易商品，如香料和各种热带产品。东亚的中华帝国，对此要求最大。[7]

在张彬村看来，"中国商人很早就在东南亚海域各个角落开展贸易，也就是传统上所说的'南海'"[8]。他们顺着季风，穿过两条"狭窄的航线"抵达南海，到每个港口搜寻天然热带产品回国，在整个地区遍访"商机"[9]。这些繁华的港口城市包括马六甲(Malacca)、亚齐(Aceh)、巴邻帝(Palembang)、班登(Banten)、安汶(Ambon)等。尽管华商贸易的遗迹随处可见，但这些地方的华人社区却并不多。而在其他地方，"中国商人只是在沿途停靠港口做生意，生意做完后就带着中国产品货物启航"[10]。经过"多个来回的交易"，他们赚得盆满钵盈，带着南海货物回到国内市场销售。张彬村提到，"在多个来回的交易中，贸易利润在不断产生和增加，而回到国内市场，他们又收获了最终也是最大的利润"[11]。

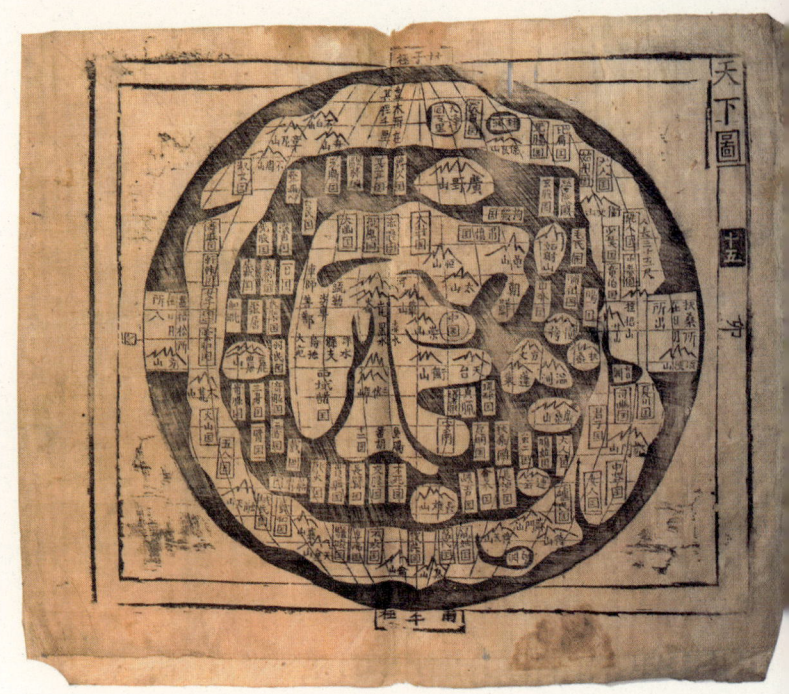

©Copyright 2010 Harris Maps – Charlottte Harris Rees

中国古代文明的传播范围，在本次展览的中国地图中清晰可见。地图收集家小亨顿·M·哈里斯博士 (Dr Hendon M Harris, Jr)《地图集》中的这些地图非常吸引人，也蕴含着迷人的现代韵味，表达了当时中国人对遥远土地和海洋的认识水平；有很多地方现在都能辨认出来。

17世纪，荷属东印度公司 (Veerenigde Oost-IndischeCompagnie, VOC 或称 Dutch East India Company) 试图控制东印度群岛，但他们却发现离不开当地华商[12]。妥善安置好华商后，荷属东印度公司占领该地区，不让其他商人进入，如印度人（他们退出这一地区）、葡萄牙人（他们当时的主要利益在澳门）、英国人、法国人、丹麦人。荷兰人把持着安汶岛(Amboina)与班达(Banda)的野丁香和肉豆蔻树及其他资源，成为他们东印度群岛商业的中流砥柱[13]。

但是，1602年VOC抵达前，"东印度整个水域甚或整个亚洲地区，都向所有商人开放"[14]。

TRADE IN THE 'SOUTH SEAS'

China, ruled by the Qing dynasty (1644–1911), was the superpower of East and South-East Asia. With a long history of trade and mercantilism dating from the Song dynasty (960–1279), the Chinese were familiar with trade commodities of the East Indies, such as spices and a large range of tropical products. It was in East Asia that imperial China had the greatest effective demand for them.[7]

As Pin-tsun Chang observed, the 'Chinese merchants were already trading in all corners of maritime Southeast Asia, an area they traditionally called the "South Seas"'.[8] They sailed with the monsoon winds on the two 'needle routes' to the South Seas, from port to port, seeking native tropical products for consumption at home and visited places throughout the region wherever 'business opportunities were available'.[9] These prosperous port cities included Malacca, Aceh, Palembang, Banten and Ambon. There were only a few Chinese communities, despite the antiquity of the Chinese trade presence. Elsewhere, 'Chinese traders just carried out their business at the ports of call and sailed away as soon as it was done' with their cargoes of Chinese products.[10] After 'many rounds of transactions', on each of which a profit was made, they returned with their cargo of South Seas commodities for sale on the Chinese home market. Chang noted that the '[p]rofit was generated and added in the many rounds of transactions, until the final and biggest profit was harvested in the home market'.[11]

The reach of the Chinese civilisation from ancient times can be seen in the Chinese maps in this exhibition. The maps from the Dr Hendon M Harris, Jr Map Collection are fascinating —and intriguingly modern— in their representation of the state of knowledge of the lands and seas beyond China; so much can be recognised.

In the 17th century, the Veerenigde Oost-Indische Compagnie (VOC) —or Dutch East India Company— sought control of the East Indies but found that the local Chinese traders were indispensable.[12] Well ensconced with them, the VOC dominated the region and excluded other traders, such as the Indians (who vacated the region), the Portuguese (whose interests in Macau came to the fore), the English, the French and the Danish. The Dutch hold on the wild clove and nutmeg trees of Amboina and Banda, in addition to other resources, was the mainstay of their commerce in the archipelago.[13]

However, until the arrival of the VOC in 1602 'the water world of the East Indies, or even the whole of Asia, was open to all participants'.[14]

Macau (at the southern tip of the Pearl River Delta, in south China) was the centre for trade in Chinese silk and Japanese silver. It was occupied by the Portuguese in 1556 and a rent was paid to China after 1573.[15] By the beginning of the 17th century, Macau reached its 'heyday' as an 'international emporium, an *entrepôt* serving three lucrative trade routes' which were monopolised by Portuguese ships.[16] However, after they were banned from trading in silver, the Portuguese lost their monopoly, which was further hastened when the Dutch displaced them at Melaka in 1641, and other competitors entered these markets.[17]

Tian Xia (World Map) from Book 1
This map was printed from wood blocks on mulberry-bark paper and is in a Korean book. Based on which cities appear on the other maps in this text, it is thought that it was produced in the late 18th century. The atlas size is 34 cm x 41 cm and the map size is 27.5 cm x 33.5 cm. The text of this style map is always in Chinese. The title 'Tian Xia,' means 'everything under heaven, or the whole earth.
From the Dr. Hendon M. Harris, Jr. Map Collection by permission of Charlotte Harris Rees, author Secret Maps of the Ancient World www.harrismaps.com

《天下图》(地图),摘自第一册。该图为桑树皮纸木刻图,取自韩语书籍。按文本其他地图中所见城市,据信该图绘于18世纪晚期。地图册大小为34x41厘米,本图大小为27.5x33.5厘米。此类地图所用文字,一般均为中文。图中所写汉字为《天下图》,意为全球地图。来自于小Hendon M. Harris博士的地图收藏,并征得《古代世界秘图》作者Charlotte Harris Rees许可。www.harrismaps.com。

CANTON AND ITS APPROACHES, MACAO

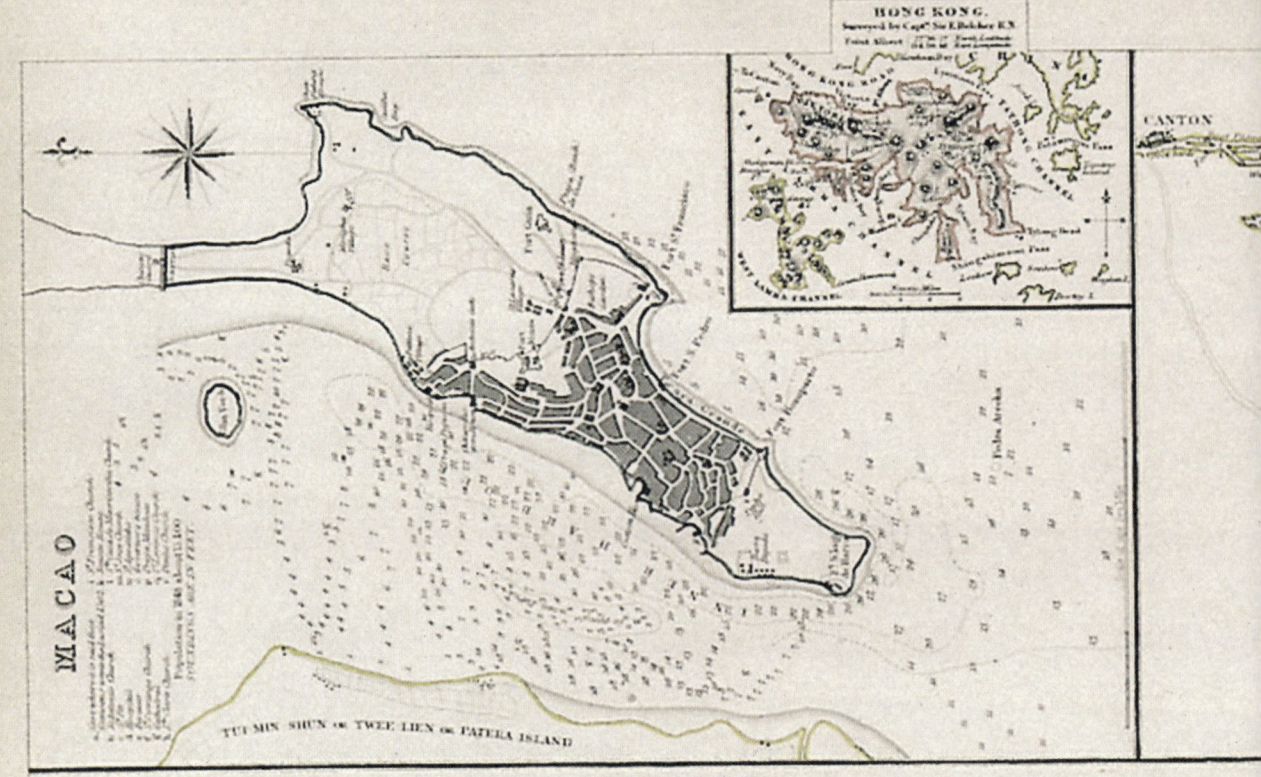

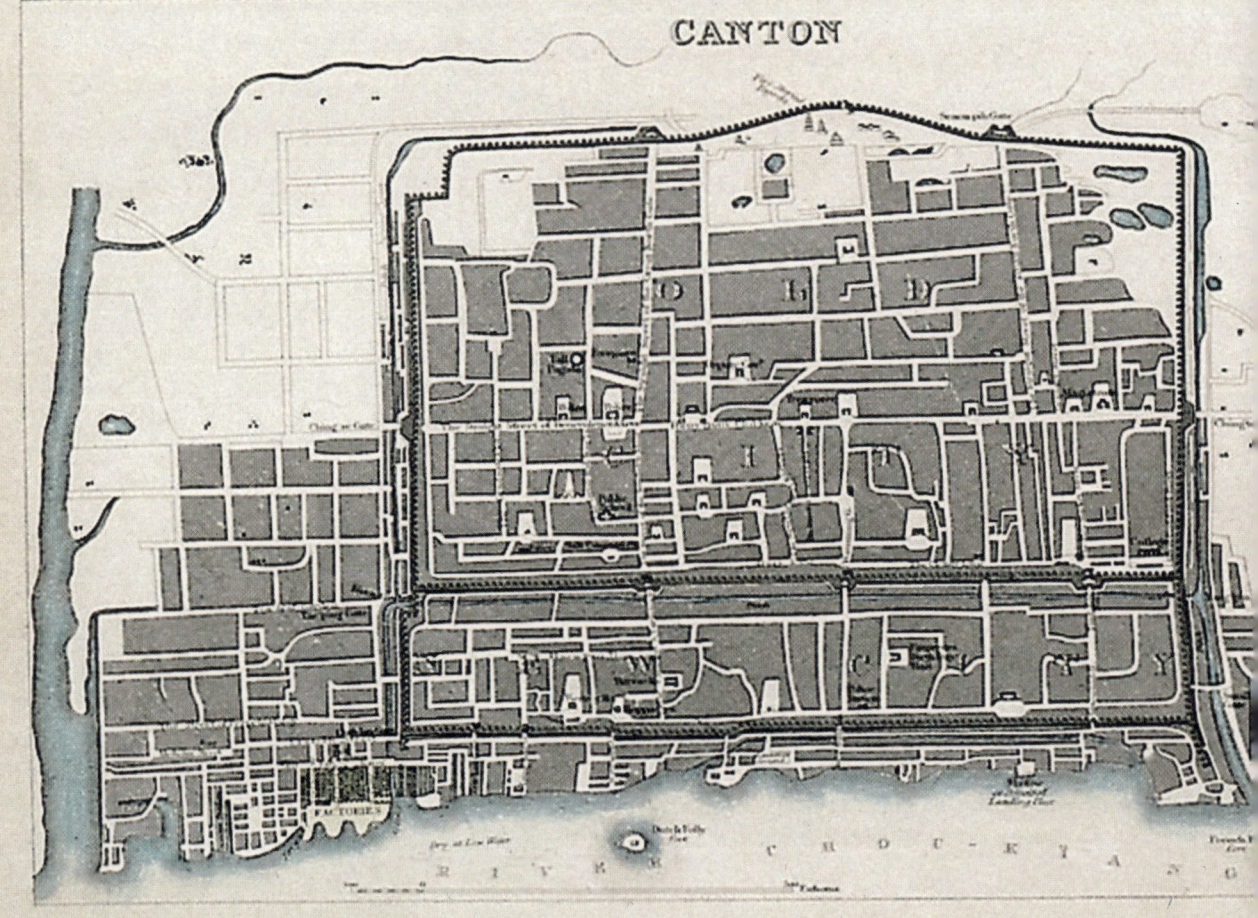

MACAO

HONG KONG.
Surveyed by Capt. Sir E. Belcher R.N.

CANTON

London, George Cox, Jan.y 1.st 1852

Canton and Its Approaches, Macao and Hong Kong - ca.1852
A fine composite sheet showing the Pearl River and its settlements in numerous details and insets, published by the Society for the Diffusion of Useful Knowledge in London from the late 1830s through to the early 1860s. The map includes a detailed survey of the Pearl River from Macao and Lantau to Guangzhou, a large detailed plan of Guangzhou, a detailed map of Macao, and a small inset map of Hong Kong Island based on the surveys of Belcher.
Courtesy of the Hong Kong University of Science and Technology.

广东及周边地区、澳门与香港 — 大约1852年

这张精美的合成地图非常详细，配有插图，绘制出珠江以及定居点。地图由伦敦实用知识传播学会在1830年代末至1860年代初出版。此地图包含对珠江从澳门和大屿山到广州段的细部测量图、一张很大的广州细部平面图、一张澳门细部，并且插入有依据所做测量的香港小地图。

香港科技大学提供。

VISTA DE LA GRAN CIUDAD DE CANTÓN

Este es el único Puerto donde permiten los Chinos(por ser feria) el comercio libre à las naciones Europeas, quatro meses al año desde gan Factorias, y Vanderas de cada nacion pero que no lleguen los Navios hasta la Ciudad

A...... Templo, y Casa del Mandarin Governador de la tierra.
B...... Casa del Opus justicia de los Chinos.
C...... Casa de alojamiento de Españoles.
D...... Factoria Dinamarquesa.
E...... Factoria Armenia.
F...... Factoria Francesa.
G...... Factoria Inglesa.
H...... Factoria Yolandesa.
I...... Factoria Sueca.
J...... Factoria Imperial.
K...... Fuerte de los Chinos.
L...... Señor que llevan en Palanqu
M...... Señora que goza del brazo
N...... Una China que lleva à cuest
O...... Un Chino que vende Perros

Vista de la gran ciudad de Canton en la China [map]. This very rare and important Spanish copperplate engraving shows the waterfront of Guangzhou. The impressive edifices of the foreign trading establishments dominate the centre of the engraving. In front of these buildings are flagpoles with each country's flags. At the bottom, a detailed lettered key identifies the principal buildings and activities.
c. 1750
Courtesy of the Hong Kong University of Science and Technology

中国广东主要城市地图【地图】

这张西班牙雕刻铜版地图极为罕见并且非常重要。地图绘出了广州的水滨地区。

外国贸易机构的宏伟大厦占据了这张雕刻地图的中心。

这些大厦的前面是一些悬挂有各国国旗的旗杆。地图底部有标明主要大厦和活动的详细图例。（大约1750年）

香港科技大学提供。

1.

1. James Moffat
View of Canton,
published in Calcutta
1802
Aquatint
Courtesy of the
British Library

2. Lieut L.G. Heath
of H.M.S. Iris
*Hong Kong &c. as seen
from the anchorage*
[map 1,2 &3]
1846
Engraving
Courtesy of the Hong Kong
University of
Science and Technology

3. E. de. Laplante
Praos Malais, Ile Java
(detail)
1846
Lithograph
nla.pic-an20806606
National Library
of Australia

4. E. de. Laplante
*Praos bouguis a la voile,
Baie Raffles ; Voiture
chinoise, Ile Banda* (detail)
1846
Lithograph
nla.pic-an20801273
National Library
of Australia

1. James Moffat
广东一览图,
加尔各答出版
1802年
凹铜版腐蚀制版
英国图书馆提供

2. H.M.S. Iris号少尉
L.G. Heath
从停泊点远眺香港
[地图1、2、3]
1846年
雕版图
香港科技大学提供

3. E. de. Laplante
Praos Malais, Ile Java
(细部)
1846年
平版印刷
nla.pic-an20806606
澳大利亚国立图书馆

4. E. de. Laplante
Praos bouguis a la voile,
Baie Raffles ; Voiture
chinoise, Ile Banda (细部)
1846年
平版印刷
nla.pic-an20801273
澳大利亚国立图书馆

2.

3.

4.

25

南中国珠江三角洲最南端的澳门是当时中国丝绸和日本银子的贸易中心。1556年，葡萄牙人占领澳门，并于1573年后向中国缴纳地租[15]。17世纪初，澳门达到了全盛时期，发展成为"国际商业中心，服务于被葡萄牙船舶垄断的三条利润丰厚贸易航线"[16]。但是，在被禁止从事银贸易后，葡萄牙人丧失了垄断地位；1641年葡萄牙人在马六甲被荷兰人击败后，这种垄断地位的丧失进一步加剧，其他竞争对手开始进入了这些市场[17]。

财大气粗的中国商人利用超级海船控制了贸易航线，而贫穷的商人，如望加锡人，则要驾着敞舱船（perahu）艰难求生。望加锡人参与印度、中国、葡萄牙和荷兰商人的国际贸易，这些外国商人都在西里伯斯岛的望加锡港建立了基地[18]。国际商人通过与地方当局及本地商人的协议，确保了自己的商品垄断地位。

望加锡商人可能会把自己的海参货物运往繁华的澳门港及中国很多港口，也会带着中国陶瓷和其他商品回来。他们一定曾在很多港口忙碌穿梭于较大商人之间。和其他人一样，他们在中国港口及驻有华人税收员的东南亚也要缴纳税收。华人是东印度公司的主要税收代理人，自1620年代起，华人的包税制就非常出名。他们数量稀少，并"建立了某种非正式寡头垄断联盟"[19]，如控制爪哇中东部的陈姓与韩姓两个家族组成了包税双头垄断联盟[20]。

18世纪初，清廷允许外国人在珠江流域的广州港经商贸易。这里迅速发展成创业中心，也几乎成为全球商业中心，其贸易税收让"北京皇帝的银库"装满了财富[21]。

但是，19世纪华商在东南亚的力量开始衰落。这里有几个原因。范·戴克 (Van Dyke) 指出，地方行政长官谨小慎微，不愿意向北京朝廷汇报太多，导致朝廷对泛亚州贸易圈的范围和性质一无所知[22]。由于对其经济状况所知甚微，北京朝廷根本没有察觉到来自大英帝国的威胁。毒品贸易、鸦片战争、银源枯竭、贸易条款不完善以及国民日益严重的骚乱动荡，促成了清王朝崩塌的加速。1834年，英国政府任命商业监督，同时行使领事与商务权，正式确立其在南中国的利益。东印度公司运势衰弱后，中国贸易被十几个独立的英国公司所接手。

随着英国对中国战略引进极易成瘾的鸦片毒品，以及'西方对茶叶和丝绸的需求渗透到沿海地区'[23]，英国的利益不断扩大。英国强迫中国按照第一次鸦片战争后签订的《1842年南京条约》，开放五个条约港口。这五个港口分别是广州、福州、宁波、厦门、上海。1842年，中国向英国割让香港；从此，由于较大型船舶被引入香港维多利亚港湾的深水港，澳门作为主要区域贸易中心的地位也在进一步衰退。

While the wealthy Chinese traders dominated the routes with superior sea craft, poor traders, such as the Macassans, earned a hard living in their small *perahu*. The Macassans were engaged in the international trade conducted by Indian, Chinese, Portuguese and Dutch traders who all established bases in Macassar, the port in the Celebes.[18] The international traders secured monopolies on commodities by agreement with local authorities and traders.

As well as many Chinese ports, the Macassans traders might have taken their cargo of trepang to the bustling port of Macau and may have returned with Chinese porcelain and other trade goods. They must have worked in many of the ports slipping in between the larger traders. They, like others, were subject to taxes, both in the Chinese ports and wherever Chinese tax collectors operated in South-East Asia. Chinese people were the VOC's major tax agents and were well known in the profession of tax farming since the 1620s. They were few and 'formed a certain informal alliance for oligopoly',[19] such as the duopoly of tax farming formed by two Chinese clans bearing the family names of Chen and Han who dominated in central and eastern Java.[20]

In the early 18th century, the Qing court allowed foreigners to trade at the port of Canton, on the Pearl River. It became a centre of enterprise and almost global commerce, and with the taxes on trade, 'the emperor's coffers in Beijing' swelled with wealth.[21]

In the 19th century, however, the Chinese trade power in South-East Asia declined. Several reasons are proffered for it. Van Dyke pointed to the cautious refusal of administrators to send their exorbitant paperwork to Beijing where there was, as a result, little understanding of the extent and nature of the pan-Asian trading ring.[22] With a poor understanding of its economic status, the dynastic powers in Beijing were oblivious to the threat from the British Empire. The drug trade, the opium wars, the silver shortage, poor terms of trade and increasing unrest among the population also contributed to the Qing dynasty's fall. From 1834, British interests in south China were formalised with the appointment by the British Government of a Superintendent of Trade who had consular as well as commercial authority. After the decline of the VOC's fortunes, the China trade was taken over by dozens of separate British companies.

British interests expanded with the strategic introduction of the highly addictive drug opium, and as '[W]estern demands for tea and silk penetrate[d] the coastal area'.[23] The British were able to force the Chinese to accede to five treaty ports under the terms of the 1842 treaty of Nanjing that concluded the First Opium War. These were Guangzhou, Fuzhou, Ningbo, Xiamen or Amoy and Shanghai. In 1842, China ceded Hong Kong to the British and Macau's position as a major regional trading centre declined further still, as a result of larger ships being drawn to the deep water port of Victoria Harbour in Hong Kong.

澳大利亚北部的望加锡人

来自世界各地和当地的商人汇聚在这片水域，在小港口竞逐商品，不时就会发生价格、合同和影响力的矛盾冲突；有时还会升级为战争。一些人认为，布顿之战(Battle of Buton)失利后，一艘望加锡敞舱船(perahu)于1666年窜逃至澳大利亚。据说也就是从这时起，望加锡人发现了海参，创建了澳大利亚的第一个出口产业。

远赴重洋的望加锡人对一些土著部落非常友好，但在澳大利亚北海岸也与其他土著部落出现暴力冲突。长久以来，他们每年来此一次。他们从西里伯斯岛往南启航，在12月或1月季风伊始抵达，然后在来年6月份顺着回风返航。在布龙·布龙的树皮画上，您会看到雨季初漫天密布的积云。这些积云呈三角形。三角云是雨季和望加锡船队来临的征兆之一，在这幅树皮画里，它们也代表着布龙·布龙的文化疆界。

早在英国人抵达澳大利亚之前，望加锡人就获得一些土著首领的批准，可以呆在特定区域捕捞海参。望加锡人把阿纳姆丛林海岸熟悉的土著领地称为马瑞格(Marege)。

他们带上"用来建造营地的现成盖屋板、铁锅、大米和其他日用品"[24]。漫长的季节里，他们在阿纳姆丛林东北部和克罗克岛 (Croker Island) 附近及其他海岸地区建立了很多营地[25]。科普兰岛(Copeland Island)、鲍恩海峡 (Bowen Strait) 北部和莱佛士港湾(Raffles Bay)都建有营地及海参加工站。人们认为，望加锡船员在格兰特岛(Grant Island)补充饮用水和蔬菜，"相传他们还用过克罗克岛明基朗(Minjilang)涌出的淡水"[26]。在一次法庭案件审理中，专家和明基朗(克罗克岛)传统业主所提供的有关这段历史的证据表明：

一些望加锡船队非常庞大。例如，在1829年，34条敞舱船(praus)满载1056个船员到访惠灵顿堡(在莱佛士港湾)。文件记载，敞舱船可装载多达60个船员。19世纪期间，行业规模不断缩小；1880年代中期后，望加锡船队通常装载100至300个人[27]。

其他加工站在这些故事里并没有提及，但其存在的证据却流传至今。约翰·布龙·布龙的先辈们与望加锡人结成联盟，并热诚欢迎望加锡船队的到来，这点在他的画里也得到了体现。在北领地首任警务署长保罗·弗尔彻 (Paul Foelsche) 的照片中，出现了海参加工站，它位于现在的科堡半岛 (Cobourg Peninsula) 上。很多地方的土著传统业主仍保存着海参灶的石头，比如梅尔维尔湾(Melville Bay) 的尼润嘎 (Nyirrnga)。望加锡

1. Drawing by HS Melville of a Macassan processing site at Port Essington on the Arnhem Land coast in 1845. In the foreground the trepang are being boiled; in the background are the smokehouses for smoking/drying the trepang. Published in The Queen, 8 February 1862.

2. Louis Le Breton France 1818–1866;
Trepang fishermen, Raffles Bay
Lithograph
National Gallery of Australia, Canberra

1. HS Melville于1845年在阿纳姆丛林海岸绘制的埃辛顿港望加锡加工点。前景里正在煮海参；背景是用来烟熏/干燥海参的熏制室。1862年2月8日刊登于《女王》报纸。

2. Louis Le Breton 法国，1818–1866年；
拉福尔湾的海参渔民
平版印刷
澳大利亚国立图书馆，堪培拉。

人将海参切开，然后煮熟、烘干、烟熏；正如本次展览的图片所示，他们在季节营地里与土著人一同工作、联姻，建立长久的友谊。他们包好加工过的海参，并带着这些珍贵的货物远赴中国港口，因为海参在那里是最畅销最昂贵的商品之一。近二百年来，望加锡人通过联姻、贸易和友谊，巩固了与澳大利亚北部及阿纳姆丛林部分地区土著人的牢固关系。望加锡的男人女人，成了雍古族人(Yolŋu)的家人，这种血缘关系也将其他望加锡人束缚在错综复杂的家庭、义务和责任网中。

THE MACASSANS IN NORTH AUSTRALIA

With traders from all the global and local powers plying these waters and competing at the small ports for commodities, prices, contracts and influence, conflicts flared from time to time, some escalating into battles. Some believe that a Macassan *perahu* fled to Australia in 1666 after defeat at the Battle of Buton. It is said that this was when the Macassan discovered the trepang and commenced Australia's first export industry.

The seafaring Macassans befriended some Aboriginal peoples, but also braved violent encounters with others on the northern coast of Australia. For long periods their visits were annual. They sailed southwards from Celebes, arriving at the beginning of the monsoon in December or January and sailing home by the following June, on the returning winds. In Bulunbulun's bark paintings, one can see the cumulus clouds that sail across the skies at the beginning of the wet season. They are represented by triangles. These triangles are a sign of the coming of the wet season and of the Macassan fleets and, in this painting, they also represent Bulunbulun's cultural boundaries.

Long before the British arrived in Australia, the Macassans obtained permission from some Aboriginal leaders to stay in particular places to harvest the trepang. The Macassans called the familiar Aboriginal territories of coastal Arnhem Land, Marege.

They brought with them 'ready-made thatch panels for camp buildings, iron boiling pots, rice and other supplies'.[24] During the long seasons, they established many camps in the northeast of Arnhem Land and also in the vicinity of Croker Island and other places along that coastline.[25] There were campsites and trepang processing stations on Copeland Island, on the north side of Bowen Strait and at Raffles Bay. It is believed that Macassan crewmen used Grant Island as a source of water and vegetable food, and 'there are oral traditions that the freshwater spring at Minjilang on Croker Island was also used by [them]'.[26] In the evidence given in a court case about this history by experts and the traditional owners of Minjilang (Croker Island), it emerged that:

Some Macassan fleets were extremely large. For example, in 1829 Fort Wellington (in Raffles Bay) was visited by 34 praus manned by 1056 men. Praus with as many as 60 crew members have been documented. The size of the industry declined throughout the 19th century and after the mid-1880s Macassan fleets generally contained between 100 and 300 men.[27]

There were other stations which have not been included in these stories, but evidence of their presence survives. John Bulunbulun's ancestors made alliances with Macassan people and, as his paintings show, welcomed their fleets. The photographs of the first Northern Territory Police Commissioner, Paul Foelsche, show the trepang processing station at what is now called Cobourg Peninsula. The stones of the trepang cooking ovens are preserved by Aboriginal traditional owners at a number of places such as at Nyirrnga in Melville Bay. The Macassans processed the trepang by splitting the animals, then cooking, drying and smoking them and, as images in the exhibition show, they worked with Aboriginal people at their seasonal camps, entered into marriages and made long term friendships. They packed the processed trepang for trade and took their precious cargo to Chinese ports where it was one of the most highly desirable and expensive commodities. For almost 200 years, the Macassans cemented strong relationships through marriage, trade and friendship with several of the Aboriginal peoples of northern Australia and parts of Arnhem Land. Macassan men and women became family members among Yolŋu clans and the kinship networks bound other Macassans in the intricate web of family, obligations and duty.

3. Eugene Ciceri, 1813–1890
Un rue de quartier Malais a Macassar, Iles Celebes 1846
Lithograph
nla.pic-an20806519
National Library of Australia

4. Wok, trepang pot with 2 handles for trepang processing (Beche-de-mer or sea cucumber), Indonesia, 16 x 58cm.
IND01280
Museum and Art Gallery of the Northern Territory

5. Urn, Macassan ceramic. Large earthenware jar or urn, normally used by macassans for water storage, 52 x 36cm.
TH92/011
Museum and Art Gallery of the Northern Territory

3. Eugene Ciceri, 1813–1890年
Un rue de quartier Malais a Macassar, Iles Celebes 1846
平版印刷
nla.pic-an20806606
澳大利亚国立图书馆

4. 加工海参使用的双耳海参锅或镬，印度尼西亚。
16 x 58cm
IND01280
北领地博物馆与艺术陈列馆

5. 望加锡陶瓷瓮。望加锡人通常用来装水的大土罐或瓮。
52 x 36cm
TH92/011
北领地博物馆与艺术陈列馆

3.

4.

5.

澳大利亚北部的英国人

遥远的南方,英国人正从澳洲殖民地南部定居点向北推进,沿途安排人开挖金矿。詹姆斯·库克船长(James Cook)于1770年代表英国王室宣布占领澳大利亚,但直到1788年,才在杰克逊港(Port Jackson)——也就是现在的悉尼——的罪犯流放地建立了第一个定居点。直到一个世纪之后,他们才控制了望加锡人到访过的北部海岸。英国人与望加锡人在这片水域的最初遭遇发生在1803年。当时英国人仍然没有绘制出澳大利亚的多数海岸,船员们都要依靠荷兰人和葡萄牙人的地图及同行们的传统知识,在澳大利亚北部海洋和海峡之间航行。

英国探险家和航海家马修·福林德斯(Matthew Flinders)是第一个环航整个澳洲大陆的英国船员,也是第一个绘制这些海岸图的英国航海家。1803年2月17日,他乘坐"调查者"(Investigator)号,在阿纳姆丛林海域遇到了一支望加锡敞舱船(perahu)船队。当时双方相互都非常猜疑和惊恐,在讲这个故事的米里亚姆·艾斯坦森(Miriam Estensen)看来,双方的这种忧惧很正常:

> 这六条敞舱船(praus)的首领是一个身材矮小的老人,名叫波巴索(Pobassoo)。他率领的这六艘船,是一支由60条船组成之船队的一个小队,整个船队归博尼王公(Rajah of Boni)所有,共载了一千多人,由一名撒鲁(Salloo)指挥。当时船队正在海岸捕捞海参(亦称bêches-de-mer)[28]。

福林德斯很想和他们交流,正巧他船上有一名厨师是马来人(可能来自现在的印度尼西亚)。虽然存在语言差异,但这名厨师还是能准确翻译出他们谈话的细节。

清晨,福林德斯带着"两名船员"(应该叫布朗(Brown)和鲍尔(Bauer))以及厨师兼翻译威廉斯登上了波巴索的船,随后六名船长也参观了"调查者"号,船员们则聚集在船边以物易物。临近中午时,又有5条敞舱船驶入这块碇泊处,"调查者"号周围聚集了越来越多的独木舟。这块独特的停泊点是海参捕捞者的海岸第一站,他们在此往竹节里倒满淡水,然后驶入卡奔塔利亚湾(Gulf of Carpentaria)[29]。

为了向波巴索船长尽可能多地了解望加锡人的活动,福林德斯把出发时间推迟了一天。他获悉,"波巴索在之前20年内已从望加锡航行至此6或7次,也是第一批来此的望加锡人"[30]。波巴索还告诉福林德斯,他们在航行期间曾遭过土著部落的暴力袭击。福林德斯注意到波巴索全副武装,他在日记里写到:"他带着两把荷兰人的小铜枪(brass gun),不过其他人却只有滑膛枪……每个马来人都佩戴着克莱斯刀(cress),即匕首"[31]。艾斯坦森这样描述这次遭遇。

> 波巴索膝盖曾被刺伤,在这次航行中,有人受了轻伤。波巴索的船上装了两门小铜炮……应船长的要求,"调查者"号炮手发了一发舰弹[32]。

天气也是一大危险。望加锡船队顺着季风航行,据福林德斯说,他们唯一的航海仪器是一个"很小的袖珍罗盘,显然是荷兰人制造的"[33]。福林德斯还记录说,前一年他们还有一艘船在海上失踪了。"调查者"号船员捡到了一个方向舵,波巴索认出那正是失踪船舶的。

THE BRITISH IN NORTH AUSTRALIA

Far to the south, the British were expanding from the southern settlements of their Australian colonies, spreading their herds and opening mines on the goldfields in their push northwards. Captain James Cook had claimed possession of Australia in 1770 on behalf of the Crown, but the first settlement was established in 1788 at the penal colony at Port Jackson, now Sydney. Not until a century later were they able to gain control of the northern coasts where the Macassans visited. The first British encounter with Macassans in these waters was in 1803. The British had still not charted much of the Australian coast and sailors relied on Dutch and Portuguese maps, and the traditional knowledge of their fraternity to navigate the seas and straits north of Australia.

The British explorer and navigator Matthew Flinders was the first British seaman to circumnavigate the continent and the first British navigator to chart these coasts. On 17 February 1803, in the *Investigator*, he met a fleet of Macassan *perahu* off Arnhem Land. There was much conjecture and consternation and, as Miriam Estensen tells the story, there was just cause for their apprehension:

> The chief of the six praus was a short, elderly man called Pobassoo. His squadron of six vessels was part of a fleet of sixty with some 1000 men, belonging to the Rajah of Boni and commanded by one Salloo, which were then on the coast diving for trepang, or *bêches-de-mer*.[28]

Flinders was keen to talk to them and, as luck would have it, on board his ship there was a Malay cook (probably from what is now Indonesia) who was able, despite their language differences, to translate precise details of their discussion:

> In the morning Flinders boarded Pobassoo's vessel with 'two of the gentlemen', presumably Brown and Bauer, and his cook-interpreter Williams, and afterwards the six captains again visited the *Investigator*, while their men gathered in canoes around the ship to barter. Just before noon five more praus sailed into the roadstead and additional canoes crowded about the *Investigator*. This particular anchorage was the trepangers' first stop on the coast, where they filled their bamboo sections with fresh water before entering the Gulf of Carpentaria.[29]

Flinders delayed his departure by a day in order to learn all he could about the Maccasans' activities from their captain Pobassoo. He learnt that 'Pobassoo had made six or seven voyages from Macassar to this coast, within the preceding twenty years, and he was one of the first who came'.[30] Pobassoo also told Flinders that during their travels they encountered violence from Aboriginal groups. Flinders observed that Pobassoo was well armed, noting in his journal that '[he] carried two small brass guns, obtained from the Dutch, but the others had only muskets … every Malay wears a cress or dagger'.[31] Estensen has written of the encounter:

> Pobassoo had once been speared in the knee and on this voyage one man had been slightly wounded. Pobassoo's vessel carried two small brass cannon … and at the captains' request the *Investigator*'s gun crew fired a carronade.[32]

The weather was also a hazard. The Macassan fleet travelled on monsoonal winds and, as Flinders stated, their only navigational instrument was a 'very small pocket compass, apparently of Dutch manufacture'.[33] Flinders also noted that the year before they had lost a vessel to the sea. The rudder of that craft was picked up by the crew of the *Investigator* and Pobassoo recognised it.

Matthew Flinders
1774–1814
General Chart of Terra Australis or Australia (cartographic material) showing parts explored between 1798 and 1803 by M. Flinders Commr of H.M.S. Investigator, 1814–1822.
nla.map-t1494
National Library of Australia

Matthew Flinders
1774–1814年
"澳大利亚总图"
（制图资料）显示了HMS调查者号指挥官M. Flinders于1798年至1803年所探索的地域，1814-1822年
nla.map-t1494
澳大利亚国立图书馆

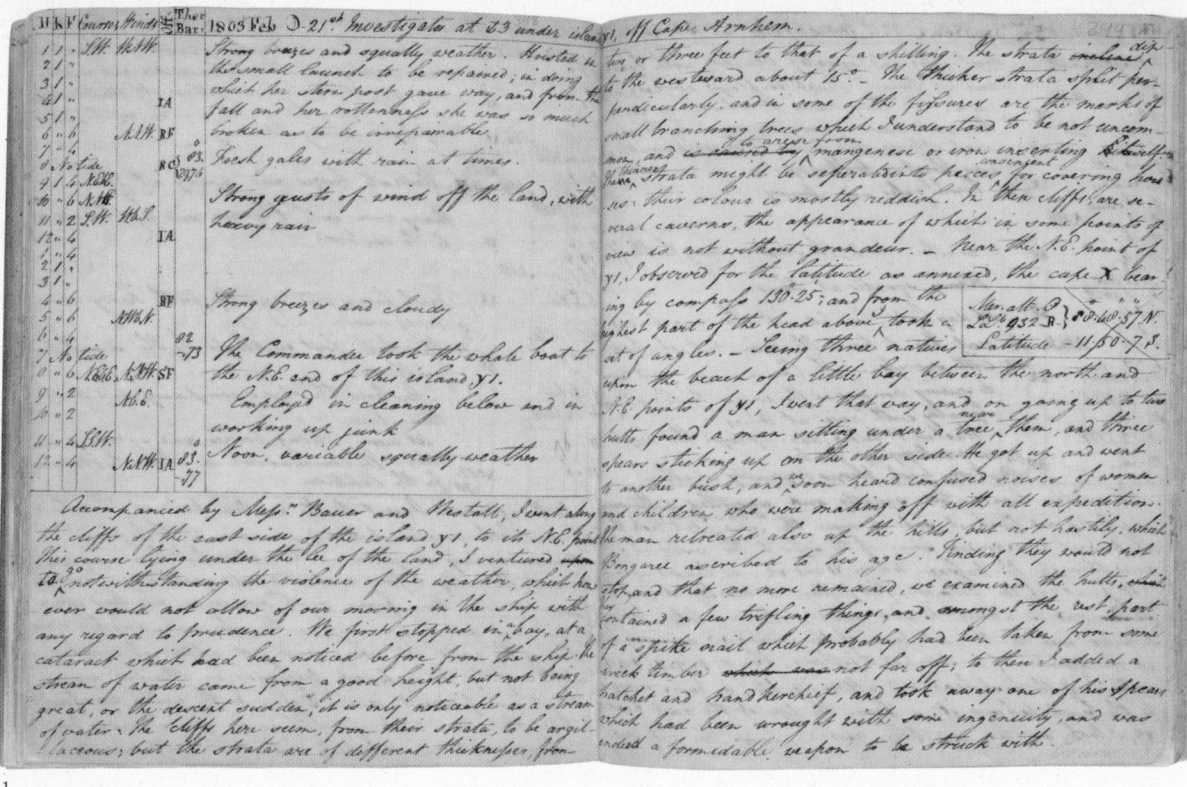

1. *Matthew Flinders - Journal on the HMS Investigator, July 1802 – June 1803* (Vol.2) February 1803. p.396-399 Mitchell Library State Library of New South Wales (A056402–A056405 inclusive)

2. William Westall 1781–1850 *The English Company's Islands, Probasso* [sic], *a Malay chief* 1803 Pencil drawing nla.pic-an4565030 National Library of Australia

2.

33

福林德斯对波巴索抽出时间介绍情况表示感谢，并送给他及其他船长"觊觎已久的铁工具，在波巴索的一再请求下，还赠送了一面英国米字旗，之后波巴索在领头船上悬挂起这面旗帜"³⁴。波巴索让他写一封信，"可能是要向以后遇到的船证明这次友好相会，于是福林德斯写了封信给波巴索，让他交给不久后可能会在海湾遇到的鲍丁（Baudin）"³⁵。为纪念此次相会，福林德斯把这段海路取名为"马来路"，而海参捕捞者赖以遮风挡雨的岛屿则被取名为"波巴索岛"³⁶。

福林德斯还在日记中描述了从波巴索口中探出的海参保鲜方法：

> 海参保鲜方法就是：将海参剖开，煮熟后压上石头；然后用竹片撑开，放在太阳下晒干，之后烟熏，完成后放入袋子里，但要经常拿出来晒太阳³⁷。

在历史学家雷吉纳·甘特（Regina Ganter）看来，福林德斯对望加锡人的兴趣可能既有商业性，又有帝国因素；望加锡人的存在则阻碍英国称霸这片殖民地。此外，福林德斯在报告中也没有提到海参贸易的商业前景，这是为了防止"蜂拥挤向北部"³⁸。甘特还提到，菲利普·帕克·金（Phillip Parker King）继续着"福林德斯"的水道测量工作（1818年至1821年），在金伯利（Kimberley）海岸遇到一支海参船队后，他还报告了望加锡与北部海岸之间频繁的贸易活动³⁹。之后，英国于1824年和1827年，先后在梅尔维尔岛及科堡半岛的莱佛士港湾建立了邓达斯堡（Fort Dundas）和惠灵顿堡（Fort Wellington），开始插手海参贸易。1828年，39团的克勒特·巴克（Collet Barker）船长在担任莱佛士港湾司令官时可能遇见了望加锡人⁴⁰。英国人想在澳大利亚北部建立一个贸易港口，一些人希望莱佛士港湾能像新加坡那样成为贸易中心。巴克任职期间，只和望加锡商人偶尔接触过，1829年他被调往乔治王海峡（King George's Sound）时，这个定居点也被废弃了⁴¹。巴克着迷于土著人的生活与文化，他抽出时间记录并编纂了"全面的姓名、词语、观察列表"⁴²。巴克几乎每天都和土著人接触，有时还连续多天与他们一同出外探险。他和具有一定声望的土著人塔拉冈（Tarragon）情同手足。这位朋友死后，他出席了葬礼，并坐在遗体脚下，"表示我对他们的同情"，并"与他们一起潸然泪下"⁴³。

1.

2.

1829年，惠灵顿堡被废弃。1839年，英国又在科堡半岛的埃辛顿港（Port Essington）建立了维多利亚定居点。1849年，这个定居点也被废弃。1874年，埃德蒙·罗宾逊（Edmund Robinson）开始在埃辛顿港开展海参贸易，1878年，他和合伙人托马斯·温菲尔德（Thomas Wingfield）在克罗克岛建立了新的海参贸易站。一些土著人在贸易站里工作，贸易站也开始取得了一定的经济成就。1879年12月，温菲尔德被土著人刺杀，罗宾逊也放弃了这个生意⁴⁴。

Flinders expressed his gratitude for taking Pobassoo's time, giving him and his captains 'coveted iron tools and, on the chief's asking for one, an "English jack, which he afterwards carried at the head of his squadron"'.³⁴ Pobassoo asked for a letter, 'presumably describing their friendly meeting, to show any other ship that he might encounter, and Flinders therefore wrote a letter for Pobassoo to give to Baudin, who could be expected in the Gulf shortly'.³⁵ Flinders commemorated the meeting naming the section of the channel Malay Road and the island in the lee of which the trepangers had sheltered, 'Pobassoo's Island'.³⁶

In his journal, Flinders also described the process of preserving trepang elicited from Pobassoo:

> The mode of preserving it is this: the animal is split down one side, boiled, and pressed with a weight of stones; then stretched open by slips of bamboo, dried in the sun, and afterwards in smoke, when it is fit to be put away in bags, but requires frequent exposure to the sun.³⁷

For the historian Regina Ganter, Flinders' interest in the Macassans might have been both commercial and imperial; Macassan presence challenged British claims to the colony. Moreover, Flinders suppressed from his reports the commercial potential of the trepang trade to avert 'a rush to the north'.³⁸ Ganter also notes that Phillip Parker King 'continued Flinders' hydrographic work (1818-21) and also reported on strong trading activities between Makassar and the north coast, having encountered a trepang fleet on the Kimberley coast'.³⁹

Thereafter, Fort Dundas at Melville Island in 1824 and Fort Wellington at Raffles Bay on the Cobourg Peninsula in 1827 were established to take advantage of the trepang trade. It is probable that Captain Collet Barker of the 39th Regiment met Macassans during his tour of duty as commandant at Raffles Bay in 1828.⁴⁰ The British wanted a trading port in the north of Australia and some hoped that Raffles Bay would become a hub for trade like Singapore. Only occasional contact with Macassan traders ensued during Barker's tenure and the settlement was abandoned when he was transferred to King George's Sound in 1829.⁴¹ Barker was captivated by Aboriginal life and culture, and spent time documenting and compiling 'a comprehensive list of names, words, and observations'.⁴² Barker had almost daily contact with Aboriginal people and sometimes accompanied them on explorations for days on end. He had befriended Tarragon, an Aboriginal man of some importance. After his friend's death, he attended to his funeral and sat at the foot of the corpse 'to shew my sympathy with them' while 'mingling my tears with theirs'.⁴³

Fort Wellington was abandoned in 1829. In 1839 the British established the Victoria Settlement at Port Essington also on the Cobourg Peninsula. This settlement was abandoned in 1849. Edmund Robinson attempted trepanging at Port Essington in 1874 and in 1878, with his partner Thomas Wingfield, he established a new trepanging station on Croker Island. A group of Aborigines worked at the station which began to achieve some financial success. In December 1879, Wingfield was murdered by Aborigines and Robinson abandoned the venture.⁴⁴

1. Samuel Middiman
1750–1831
View of Malay Road from Pobassoo's Island
Published Feb.12, 1814
Engraving
nla.pic-an7746516
National Library of Australia

2. Emile Lassalle
1813–1871
Port Essington, cote n. de l'Australie 1846
Lithograph
nla.pic-an7851127
National Library of Australia

1. Samuel Middiman
1750–1831年
从Pobassoo岛远眺马来路景观
1814年2月12日出版
雕版图
nla.pic-an7746516
澳大利亚国立图书馆

2. Emile Lassalle
1813–1871年
埃辛顿港，cote n. de l'Australie，1846年
平版印刷
nla.pic-an7851127
澳大利亚国立图书馆

土著与望加锡人的一些冲突

武辛·邓·兰卡（Using Daeng Rangka）（1845年？至1927年）是澳大利亚北部望加锡海参捕捞业的一名船长（也就是麦克奈特所称的戴辛邓·曼兰卡（Desindaeng Manrangka）），他出生在西里伯斯岛南部的勒巴康（Labbakang）。他的父亲是布吉人（Bugis），母亲是望加锡人。儿时，武辛就和每年一度的船队一同来过澳大利亚。1883年12月，尽管心不甘情不愿，他还是成为第一个就敞舱船博登·波特拉号（Bondeng Patola）而向南澳大利亚州政府购买海参捕捞许可证的船长[45]。1886年至1887年的捕捞季期间，他的伊冉·博陵号（Erang Poleang）在梅尔维尔岛失事。他"用一把旧卡宾枪"击退了土著人的攻击，"直到四条独木舟赶来"方才脱险[46]。三周后，三条独木舟抵达，并露出他们在鲍恩海峡税收站发生过冲突的迹象，他们在此曾获得大米，后又继续东进。

1887年起，武辛指挥了一条新的更大型的博登·波特拉号。1895年3月，"他再次在卡奔塔利亚湾西海岸失事"。3周后，"武辛乘坐独木舟跋涉400英里（644公里）抵达鲍恩海峡"[47]。在申请退还失事敞舱船(perahu)缴纳的47英镑未遂后，"北领地海关基层征收员阿尔佛雷德·西塞(Alfred Searcy)说武辛'很诚实，一贯乐意缴纳税项'"[48]。1899年，政府派出的小组在梅尔维尔湾意外发现了武辛。他坚称自己是因为损坏了主桅才无法前往鲍恩海峡，但仍然缴纳了更多的许可费和税费[49]。

1890年代末起，武辛似乎经常指挥班嘎·伊佳亚号（BungaEjaya），也称为博恩卡瓦·印佳亚号（Boenkawa Injaya）。1906年，南澳大利亚州政府突然决定禁止望加锡人，而让当地企业受益，为此，企业家普度（Poeddoe）（有时也拼写为Puddu）·邓·唐博（Daeng Tompo）选择武辛来确认这一报告的真伪。由此，武辛目睹了这个具有200年历史之产业的衰败，也成为最后一个从望加锡远赴澳大利亚的海参捕捞船长[50]。某敞舱船(perahu)中所存他的望加锡手稿签字，"充分证明他有文化，了解相关政府规定"[51]。损失了两条船以及整个行业中存在最终的问题，让他无法从远航中挣得太多财富。

1907年从澳大利亚回到故土后，他又航行到小巽他群岛（Lesser Sunda Islands），之后就在望加锡的马洛库村（Kampong Maloku）安度晚年。武辛的首任妻子是一个名叫巴思（Basse）的望加锡女人，没有生育子女；第二任妻子邓·特楠(Daeng Tanang)也是望加锡人，为他生了11个孩子。其中一个名叫曼根格莱·邓·马洛（Mangngellai Daeng Maro）的儿子，在最后两次航行中陪同他前往澳大利亚。据说在阿纳姆丛林东部，还有一个土著女人为他生了2个女儿和1个儿子。那个地区的土著人仍然记得他的名字。1927年，他在马洛库村去世[52]。

SOME ABORIGINAL–MACASSAN ENCOUNTERS

A captain in the Macassan trepanging industry of northern Australia, Using Daeng Rangka (1845?–1927) (referred to by Macknight as Desindaeng Manrangka) was born at Labbakang in south Celebes. He was the son of a Bugis father and a Macassarese mother. Using first came to Australia with the annual fleet as a small boy. In December 1883, he was the first captain to purchase, most unwillingly, a South Australian Government trepanging licence for the *perahu* under his command, *Bondeng Patola*.[45] He was wrecked on Melville Island during the 1886–1887 season aboard the *Erang Poleang*. He fended off an attack by Aboriginals 'with an old carbine until four dug-out canoes were launched'.[46] Three weeks later, three of the canoes arrived showing signs of the encounter at Bowen Strait revenue station, where they were given rice to continue eastward.

From 1887, Using commanded a new and larger *Bondeng Patola*. In March 1895 'he was again wrecked, on the western coast of the Gulf of Carpentaria'. In the three weeks that followed 'Using made a 400-mile (644 km) trip in canoes to Bowen Strait'.[47] In an unsuccessful application for the refund of £47 paid by the wrecked *perahu*, 'Alfred Searcy, sub-collector of customs for the Northern Territory, described Using as "honest and always willing to pay [his] duties"'.[48] In 1899 Using was by chance discovered in Melville Bay by a government party. He insisted that the loss of his mainmast had kept him from Bowen Strait but paid the greater part of his licence fee and duty.[49]

From the late 1890s Using seemed to have regularly commanded the *Bunga Ejaya*, or *Boenkawa Injaya*. In 1906 the South Australian Government sudden decision to prohibit the Macassans in favour of local enterprise prompted the entrepreneur Poeddoe (sometimes spelt Puddu) Daeng Tompo to choose him to check the truth of the report. Using, thus, saw the decline of the 200-year-old industry and was the last of the trepanging captains from Macassar to visit Australia.[50] His signature in Macassarese script preserved on a *perahu* manifest 'shows that he was literate and aware of the relevant government regulations'.[51] The loss of two vessels and the final problems of the industry make it unlikely that he earned much money from his voyages.

After his return from Australia in 1907 he completed one further voyage to the Lesser Sunda Islands and then retired to Kampong Maloku in Macassar. Using's first marriage to a Macassarese woman named Basse' was childless; his second wife Daeng Tanang, also Macassarese, bore him eleven children. A son, Mangngellai Daeng Maro, accompanied him to Australia on his two last voyages. Using is also said to have had two daughters and a son by an Aboriginal woman in eastern Arnhem Land. His name is still remembered by Aboriginals in that area. He died at Kampong Maloku in 1927.[52]

Photographer unknown
Alfred Searcy in the Northern Territory c.1882
Image courtesy of the State Library of South Australia
(PRG 280/1/43/505)

摄影:未知
Alfred Searcy在北领地,大约1882年
图片承蒙南澳州立图书馆提供
(PRG 280/1/43/505)

邓·撒落(Daeng Sarro)

邓·撒落是一支海参捕捞船队的望加锡船长，1950年前后他还住在望加锡南部的邦投兰努(Bontorannu)村里。他向荷兰学者森思(A Cense)博士及其印度尼西亚籍同事阿卜杜兰辛(Abdurrahim)叙述了海参捕捞者们从望加锡到澳大利亚再沿着澳洲海岸的航线[53]。这段叙述的重要意义在于，它是基于印象深刻的个人经历，涉及了与其所谓之土著"首领"之间的重要关系。此外，他还说一些土著人很好斗的故事，还有一些土著人则是相知甚稔的好友，比如他下面的叙述：

> 又过了一天，我们到了克兰·曼根间巴(Karaeng Mangngemba)，这里有一片美丽的白沙滩一直延伸向东，还有木麻黄树，当地人非常好斗。又航行几天后，我们抵达曼恩斯(Ma'ne's)湾和申福来(Sandfly)湾。在这两个地方，当地人都很不友善（这些地方可能都在梅尔维尔岛）。过了申福来湾，我们又航行一天来到马德(Mud)湾——靠近唐角(Cape Don)，之后再过半天就到里夫(River)湾（海参湾）。这个地区的人们非常友好，男人们都愿意到船上工作，收集海参来换取食物和烟草。
>
> 然后我们会往南、往东南航行到旁疆湾(Pandjang Bight)——澳拉利(Aurari)湾、瓦伊拉(Waira)大岛——北高奔(North Goulburn)岛，之后就到了普阿林嘎(Pua'Rengga')——布雷斯威特角(Braithwaite Point)，这个定居点人口很多，首领名叫曼博罗纳(Mamborona)。他的孙子盖米(Gammi)、班塔拉(Buntala')和蒙多(Mondo)也曾经和我一起返航到望加锡[54]。

据麦克奈特观察，邓·撒落多次前往澳大利亚，都是出于商业目的：收集和储存海参，销往中国市场[55]。这样做的后果就是要经常与当地土著部落打交道；在同伴中，邓·撒落对土著人的了解可能最有代表性。这一点在邓·撒落详细准确的航行叙述中做了清楚说明：

> 从这里往南，就可以到所谓的博德莱教父区(Father Birdlime)——邓达斯山(Mount Dundas)，这附近有个地方叫阔玛(Kormar)[迈尔斯(Miles)岛]，再过去就是巴帕(Bapa')湾——布拉德尚(Bradshaw)港，那里有个定居点叫卡坎噶(Karkarnga)。这里还有个岛，是很出名的海参炉——沃博理纳(Wobalinna)岛。有个地方叫卡瑞恩·曼根格莱(Karaeng Mangngellai)湾——格雷斯(Gray's)湾，那里的首领名叫昂够帕(Onggopa)，船队经常在这里逗留一个月。这里有三个营地，我们分别称之为"大罗望子树(Big Tamarind Tree)"、"仁岗(Renggang)村"和"栋浦(Dompu)村"。在嘉瓦(Djawa')湾——特莱尔(Trial)湾的一些暗礁里，也可以捕捞到海参。之后我们经常会在邓·门图(Daeng Muntu')岛——武达(Woodah)小岛上呆半个月。再往南，就是内尔教父(Father Nail)营地，在新湾(New Bay)附近有一条狭窄的海峡。

1.

2.

DAENG SARRO

Daeng Sarro was a Macassan captain of a trepang fleet, who, in about 1950 was still living in the village of Bontorannu just south of Macassar. He recounted the route followed by the trepangers, from Macassar to Australia and then along its coast, to Dutch scholar Dr A Cense and his Indonesian associate, Abdurrahim.[53] The significance of the account is that it is based on well remembered personal experiences which include important relationships with Aboriginal 'chiefs', as he referred to them. Moreover, he described some Aboriginal people as aggressive and others as well-known friends, for instance in the following:

Another day further on was Karaeng Mangngemba, a place which had a beautiful white beach stretching away to the east and a row of casuarina trees, and where the natives were very aggressive. Another days' sailing brought us to Ma'ne's Bay and Sandfly Bay. At both these places the native people were unfriendly [*All these places are probably on Melville Island*]. Beyond Sandfly Bay, we sailed for a day to Mud Bay [*near Cape Don*] and then for half a day to River Bay [*Trepang Bay*]. In this area, the people were peaceful and the men prepared to work on board the ships, collecting trepang in return for food and tobacco.

Then we would sail south sou'east to Pandjang Bight [*Aurari Bay*], Waira [*North Goulburn Island*] a large island, then to Pua'Rengga' [*Braithwaite Point*] a populous settlement whose chief was called Mamborona. This man's grandsons, Gammi, Buntala' and Mondo, once sailed back to Macassar with me.[54]

The reason for Daeng Sarro's many visits to Australia, as Macknight observes, was commercial: to collect and preserve the trepang to sell in the Chinese market.[55] The outcome was a sustained engagement with local Aboriginal groups. Daeng Sarro was probably typical of most of his companions in his knowledge of them. This is evident in Sarro's detailed and precise account of his travels:

Sailing southward from here, one reached the area known as Father Birdlime [*Mount Dundas*] with a place called Kormar [*Miles Island*] nearby, and then Bapa' Bay [*Port Bradshaw*], where there was a settlement called Karkarnga. Here too, lay the island known as the Fireplaces for Boiling the Trepang [*Wobalinna Island*]. At a place called the Bay of Karaeng Mangngellai [*Gray's Bay*], where the local chief was called Onggopa, the fleets used to stay for a month. Here there were three camps known as the Big Tamarind Tree, Renggang village and Dompu village. In Djawa' Bay [*Trial Bay*], trepang was also gathered from a certain reef. Next we used to spend a fortnight on the island of Daeng Muntu' [*Isle Woodah*]. Farther to the south lay the camp Father Nail and a narrow strait near New Bay.[56]

1–2. Groote Eylandt Rock Art
Courtesy of Anindilyakwa Land Council and the Museum and Art Gallery of the Northern Territory

1–2. 格鲁特岛岩画
安尼迪利亚克瓦土地委员会以及北领地博物馆与艺术陈列馆提供

直至罗宾逊在埃辛顿港建立海参营地前,"望加锡人实质上已垄断了阿纳姆丛林西北部的海参"[57]。虽然当地海参捕捞者的活动"没有带来直接竞争",但也"间接影响了望加锡人的海参产业"[58]。

1884年,南澳大利亚州政府开始向望加锡敞舱船(perahu)征税,而教会团体的其他措施给本已贫困不堪的望加锡海参捕捞者带来了更大的负担[59]。税费为"起始的20吨每吨10先令,之后每吨5先令"[60]。这些法规于1882年6月30日审批通过,"成为1872年法案的框架"[61]。

1906年,南澳大利亚州政府采纳了"整个海岸都应禁止望加锡人[62]"的建议,主要目的在于保护和鼓励本地产业[63]。本已势弱的望加锡敞舱船(perahu)也因此被迫放弃每年一度远赴澳大利亚的做法。

即使一个多世纪后的今天,雍古族人仍然记得当年望加锡人来此的情景。这些故事通过口叙、歌舞、树皮画以及在交流过程中产生的转化型文化遗产而代代相传。尽管现代南苏拉威西人对土著人几乎一无所知,但当地很多民歌仍在歌颂着当初远赴马瑞格(Marege)及其他更遥远地区的航海壮举[64]。考古和民族历史研究方面的证据表明,"海参贸易是丰富多样的群岛间贸易系统中一个不可或缺的组成部分,而17世纪起的北澳大利亚航海之旅,进一步扩大了贸易网络"[65]。

土著人不吃海参,他们认为没有经过加工的海参是有毒的[66]。但望加锡人带来了精彩的贸易机会,这些机会与在宗教典礼上交换石器、石斧和各类物品的宗教贸易传统产生了共鸣。

望加锡人以衣服、烟草、刀具、大米、鸦片和酒等商品,向土著人换取在当地部落地盘上捕捞海参的权利;借助土著劳动力参与捕捞和加工海参;及换取建立海参加工营地及获取淡水的权利。土著人也用螺壳、龟壳、小粒珍珠、珍珠贝来交易,自19世纪后期起,水牛角也成为交易商品之一。望加锡人还带来了铁器和武器。铁斧,亦称"战斧",就用来制作独木舟力帕力帕(lipalipa),这大大提高了独木舟在河流和海岸的航行速度。[67]

在了解了亘古不灭的血缘关系后,一些土著人也跟随望加锡人重返戈瓦王国。

雷吉纳·甘特认为,望加锡人"不仅仅是访客,他们经常来到同一个地方,呆上几个月,有时住上一整年"[68]。有关望加锡人来此活动的考古证据遍及澳大利亚北海岸和历史书:"他们挖井造屋,给各个地方命名,有些地名也被雍古族所采纳"[69]。从山山水水到雍古族人的歌曲,他们深深地烙刻了历史印迹。甘特提到,"望加锡苏丹王宫里有一份特殊的地图……上面表明了'戈瓦王国及1660年前一直接受戈瓦主权之地区'的边界"[70]。据甘特称,这份地图表明望加锡处在这个包含澳大利亚北部在内之王国的中心。土著人自己是否接受了戈瓦主权的统治和主张,这一点让人疑惑;而这一点在证明他们与戈瓦远航公民关系的证据里,也没有得到体现。总之,没有证据表明马瑞格(Marege)早在1660年就有望加锡人的身影。因此,主权一说是否真实存在,尚待认真论证。证据表明的不是占领与征服的关系,而是平等和尊重的关系。

THE MACASSAN LEGACY
AFTER THE END OF THE TRADE

Until Robinson established the trepang camp at Port Essington, 'Macassans maintained a virtual monopoly over the trepang from north western Arnhem Land'.[57] Even though the activities of local trepangers offered 'little direct competition' they 'indirectly impacted on the Macassan industry'.[58]

The introduction of taxes levied against Macassan *perahu* in 1884 by the South Australian Government and other actions by missionary groups imposed even greater burdens on the already impoverished Macassan trepangers.[59] Taxes levied were '10/- per ton for the first twenty tons and 5/- per ton thereafter'.[60] These regulations were approved on 30 June 1882 and 'framed under the act of 1872'.[61]

In 1906, primarily in order to protect and encourage local industry,[62] the South Australian Government acted on recommendations that the 'whole of the coast should be closed to the Macassans'.[63] The already dwindling Macassan *perahu* were thereby forced to abandon their annual visits to Australia.

Even after the passage of over a century since the end of the trade, the Yolngu people still remember the visits today. The stories are related through oral history, songs and dances, and bark paintings as well as the cultural legacy of transformations that resulted from the contact. Although the people in modern day southern Sulawesi may know little about Aboriginal peoples, there are local folk songs which celebrate epic voyages to Marege and other far away places.[64] Archaeological and ethno-historical evidence suggests that 'trepanging was an integral part of the rich and diverse inter-archipelago trade system and that from the 17th century the voyages to northern Australia were an expansion of a larger trading network'.[65]

Aboriginal people did not eat trepang; they believed it was poisonous — which it is without processing.[66] But the Macassans offered exciting trade opportunities which resonated with the existing ritual trade traditions associated with stone tools, stone adzes and various objects exchanged at ceremonies.

Macassan goods such as cloth, tobacco, knives, rice, opium and alcohol were traded with Aboriginal people in exchange for the rights to harvest the trepang in local clan estates; for Aboriginal labour to aid in the harvesting and processing of trepang; and for rights to establish trepang processing camps and to access fresh water. Aboriginal people also traded goods, such as bailer shells, turtle shells, seed pearl, pearl shells and, from the late 19th century on, buffalo horns. The Macassans also brought iron tools and weapons. The iron axe or 'tomahawk' was used to make *lipalipa* or dugout canoes, much improving their ability to travel quickly along rivers and along the coasts.[67]

Some Aboriginal people travelled back to the Kingdom of Gowa with the Macassan in acknowledgement of the enduring kinship ties.

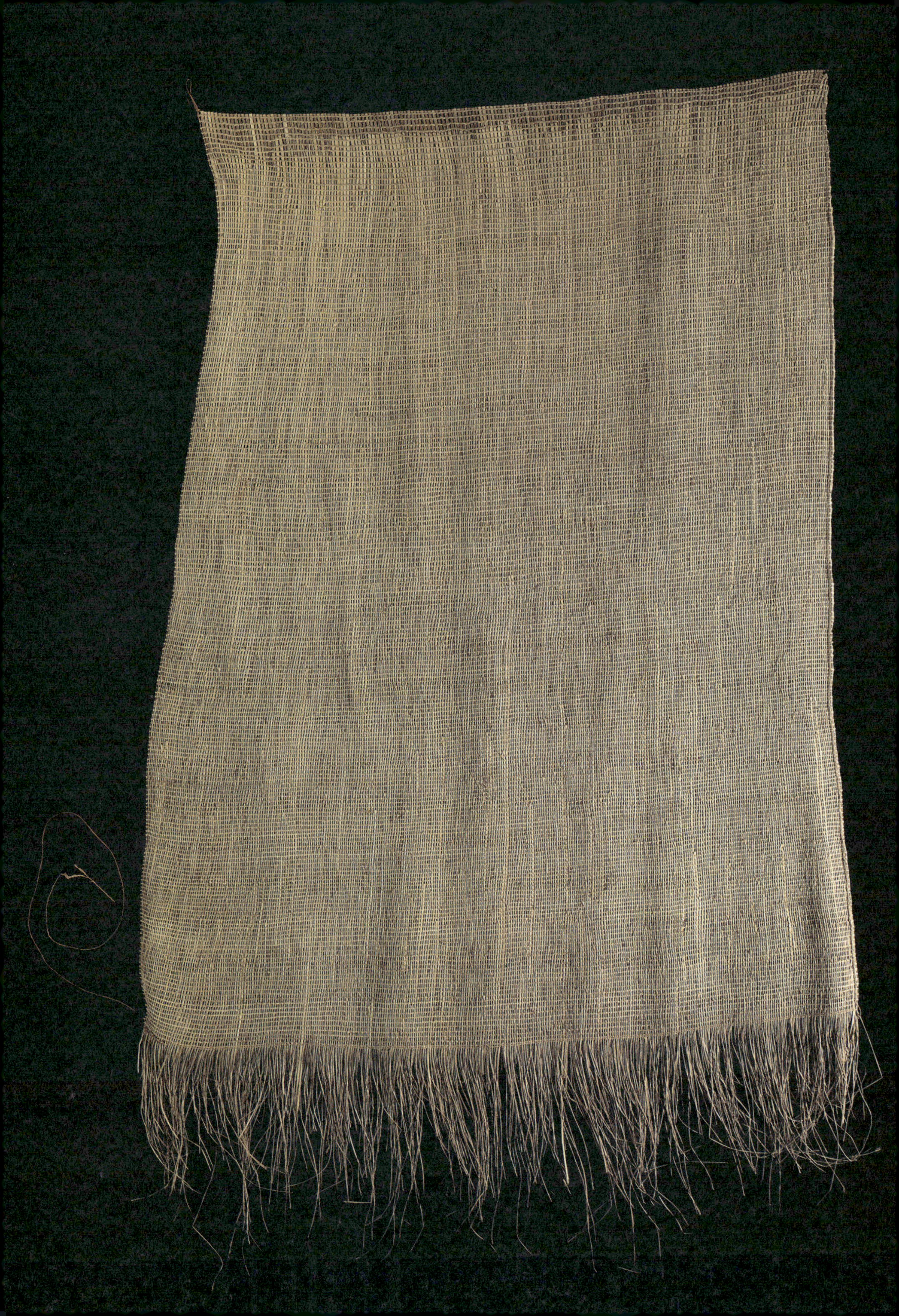

Regina Ganter noted of the Macassans that '[t]hey were more than visitors, coming regularly to the same places, staying for several months or sometimes a whole year'.[68] The archaeological evidence of their presence and activities abounds along Australia's northern coastlines and in the history texts; 'they dug wells and erected dwellings and named places, some of which became adopted by Yolŋu'.[69] Their imprint extends from the landscape to the song cycles of the Yolŋu people. Ganter referred to an 'extraordinary map at the Sultan's Palace in Macassar … which shows the boundaries of the "Gowanese kingdom and areas that accepted Gowanese sovereignty until 1660"'.[70] According to Ganter, the map shows Macassar is at the centre of the kingdom that includes the north of Australia. It is doubtful that Aboriginal people themselves accepted the domination and assertion of sovereignty of Gowa; and there is no indication of such in the evidence of their relationship with its seafaring citizens. In any case, there is no evidence that there were Macassans in Marege as early as 1660. Whether this assertion of sovereignty was in any way real is a matter of speculation. The evidence shows not a relationship of domination and subjection, but rather one of equality and respect.

Opposite.
Happy Wudjarra
Moiety: Unconfirmed
Clan: Unconfirmed
Canoe sail c.1988
Pandanus
313 x 193cm
X91096
Museum Victoria

42頁
Happy Wudjarra
半族：未证实
部落：未证实
独木舟帆，大约1988年
潘达洛斯
313 x 193cm
X91096
维多利亚州博物馆

1. *Sail Making:*
Woman making a
sail of pandanus leaf.
Crocodile Islands
North Eastern Arnhem Land,
Northern Territory
September 1935
Photograph by
D.F. Thomson.
Courtesy of Mrs D.M.
Thomson and Museum
Victoria

2. *Watercraft: Dugout canoe.*
Wänguri mättä
Arnhem Land,
Northern Territory
7th September 1935
Photograph by D.F. Thomson.
Courtesy of Mrs D.M.
Thomson and Museum
Victoria

1. 制作船帆：用露兜树叶制作船帆的妇女。
鳄鱼岛。
北领地阿纳姆丛林东北部
1935年9月
摄影：D.F. Thomson
D.M. Thomson夫人和维多利亚州博物馆提供

2. 船：独木舟。
北领地阿纳姆丛林
Wänguri mättä
1935年9月7日
摄影：D.F. Thomson。
D.M. Thomson夫人和维多利亚州博物馆提供

1. Unknown artist
Macassan style pipe
Wood, natural pigments
30.8 x 2.5cm
ABETH-2848
Museum and Art Gallery
of the Northern Territory

2. Unknown artist
Luniny or Bamutuka
Wood
Central Arnhem Land
51.2 x 3cm
ABETH-2060
Museum and Art Gallery
of the Northern Territory

3. Unknown artist
Lungay
Wood, bullet shell case
for the bowl
Yirrkala, North Eastern
Arnhem Land
59.3 x 2.1cm
ABETH-2014
Museum and Art Gallery
of the Northern Territory

4. Unknown artist
Macassan style pipe
Wood, natural pigments
North East Arnhem Land
55 x 3.6cm
ABETH-2862
Museum and Art Gallery
of the Northern Territory

5. Unknown artist
Muruku-Unga: Kwitanga
Ochred macassan pipe
Wooden stem with burnt
dot design wooden bowl
Bathurst and Melville
Islands
73 x 4cm
ABETH-0184
Museum and Art Gallery
of the Northern Territory

6. Unknown artist
Smoking pipe
Wood, incised pattern
Yirrkala, North Eastern
Arnhem Land
66.5 x 4.5 x 3cm
X44236
Museum Victoria

1. 无名艺术家
望加锡式烟管
木质，天然色素
30.8 x 2.5cm
ABETH-2848
北领地博物馆和美术馆

2. 无名艺术家
Luniny木或Bamutuka木
阿纳姆丛林中部
51.2 x 3cm
ABETH-2060
北领地博物馆和美术馆

3. 无名艺术家
Lungay
木质、子弹壳烟锅
阿纳姆丛林东北部Yirrkala
59.3 x 2.1cm
ABETH-2014
北领地博物馆和美术馆

4. 无名艺术家
望加锡式烟管
木质，天然色素
阿纳姆丛林东北部
55 x 3.6cm
ABETH-2862
北领地博物馆和美术馆

6. 无名艺术家
烟袋
木质，刻花式
阿纳姆丛林东北部
Yirrkala
66.5 x 4.5 x 3cm
X44236
维多利亚州博物馆

5. 无名艺术家
Muruku-Unga: Kwitanga
赭色望加锡烟管
木枝，点烫设计烟锅
Bathurst和Melville岛屿
73 x 4cm
ABETH-0184
北领地博物馆和美术馆

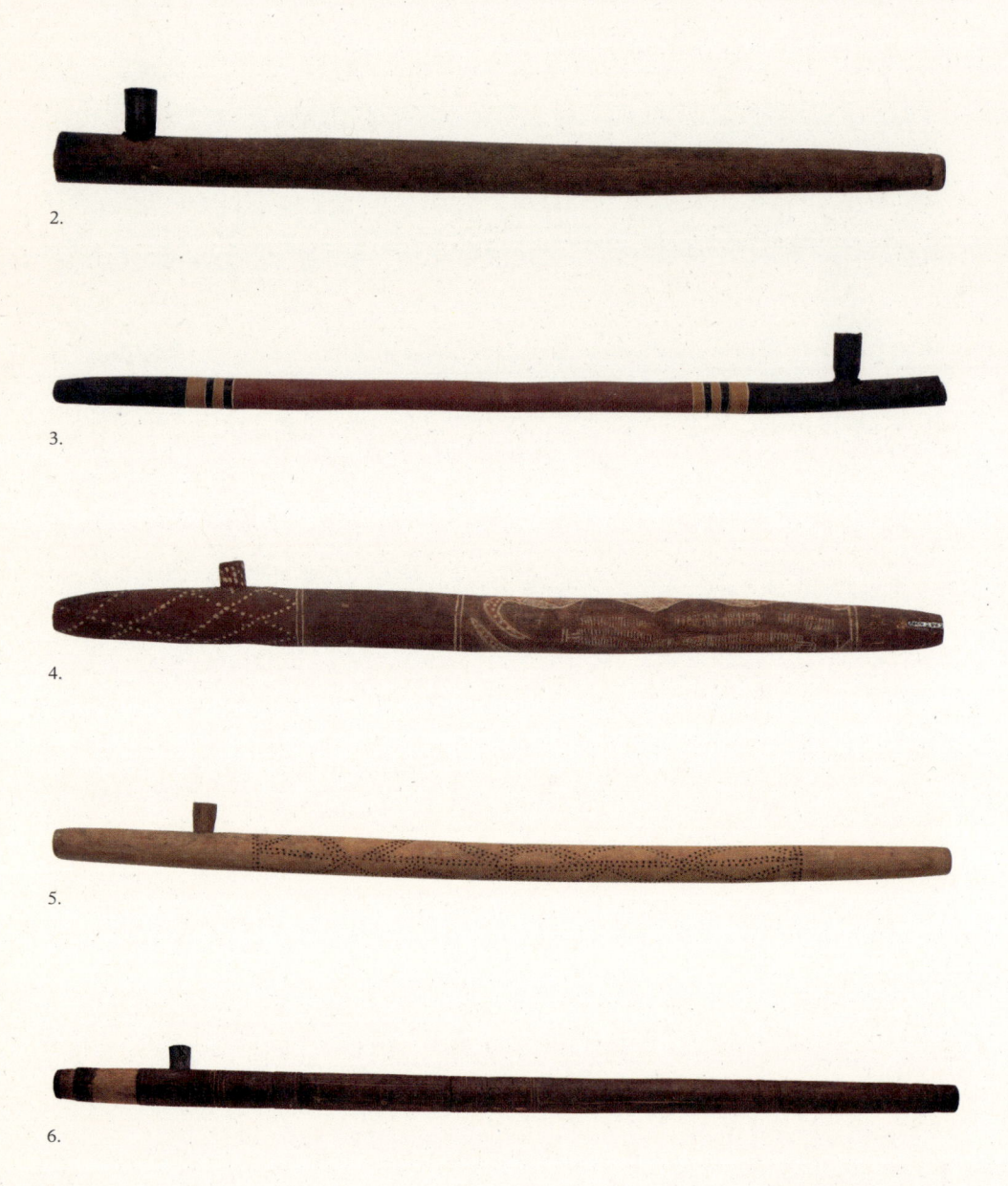

Axel Poignant 1906–1986
Narrana smoking a Macassan pipe, Liverpool River Region, Northern Territory ca. 1952
nla.pic-vn4422663
National Library of Australia

Axel Poignant 1906–1986
Narrana抽望加锡管
北领地利物浦河地区
约1952年
nla.pic-vn4422663
澳大利亚国立图书馆

Crab claw smoking pipes, Maningrida, Central Arnhem Land
Dimensions variable
ABETH-0750
ABETH-2730 A–C
Museum and Art Gallery of the Northern Territory

蟹爪烟袋
阿纳姆丛林中部Maningrida
大小各异
ABETH-0750
ABETH-2730 A–C
北领地博物馆和美术馆

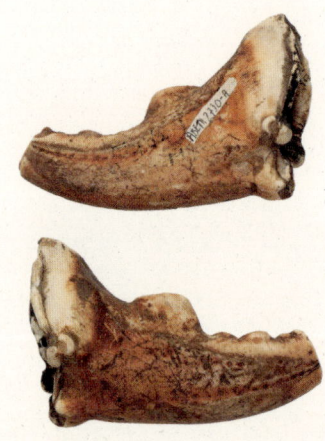

Smoking pipe - crab claw.
Wanguri Clan, Arnhem Bay,
North East Arnhem Land
c.1935
Photograph by D.F.
Thomson.
Courtesy of Mrs D.M.
Thomson and Museum
Victoria

烟袋——蟹爪.
阿纳姆丛林东北部阿纳姆湾
Wanguri部落
约1935年
摄影：D.F. Thomson.
D.M. Thomson夫人和维多
利亚州博物馆提供

望加锡人和海参贸易在当今土著文化传统里的共鸣

可能在二百多年前的某一天,雨季雨水渐少,海上风平浪静,地平线上出现了巨大的三角云,突然,在独木舟上捕鱼的土著人看到远处出现了形状奇特的物体。他们可能会等着看看这些到底是什么东西,看着这些物体慢慢在波涛上起伏航行,一路驶向陆地。最初见面时,他们可能很小心翼翼,若来客索要淡水,那么可能就会成为双方友谊的开始。这就是土著人后代和望加锡人后代用望加锡语及古帕朋古(Gupapuyngu)语演绎的戏剧《海参》里所讲述的故事[71]。表演中几乎没有掺入任何情感。这是在用这类故事开端的兴奋和浪漫情怀,以粗野而幽默的方式来讲述他们首次相遇的紧张情绪。舞台上,望加锡人冒着大风暴抵达这里,他们亟需淡水。第一节表演的精彩之处,是古帕朋古人用时尚方式,表演了喝下望加锡人带来的第一瓶楠纳基(nganaji)(雍古族人对荷兰大茴香酒的叫法)后突然喝醉的醉态。他们还表演了用长烟管抽烟及武术对决。这些缠绵故事讲述了一段浪漫的"爱情交易",叙述了一名雍古族女孩与一名向其父亲买亲的望加锡船员相遇的故事[72]。《海参》里演奏的雍古族歌曲"充斥着悲伤,控诉着望加锡时代诱拐和强迫买卖雍古族妇女的故事"[73]。利萨·帕尔默(Lisa Palmer)这样评价这段跨文化故事,"望加锡的商品给雍古族带来了利益和骚乱。事实证明,刀具和酒精都会致命,尤其是在对诱拐雍古族妇女的行为付诸愤怒的报复时。[74]"这个戏剧还体现了雍古族与望加锡的血缘关系。"望加锡男一号演员曼苏尔(Mansjur)的爷爷奥钦·邓·兰卡(Otching Daeng Rangka)是一名望加锡船长,当年他诱拐并娶了在《海参》里出任雍古族大祭司的玛丘维(Matjuwi)的曾祖母"[75]。这类关系很被看重,深受雍古族人的尊重。而在阿纳姆丛林,这个戏剧也让人"回想戈瓦王国的辉煌过去,以及一度位于东印度群岛贸易航线中心的港口城市望加锡的航海实力"[76]。

对很多土著人而言,望加锡时代留下了一段特征鲜明的文化和历史传奇。例如,望加锡语成了澳大利亚北海岸很多地区的通用语言(lingua franca)。这种语言不仅用来和望加锡海参商人交易,在偏远的土著人群中还用来雇佣望加锡人。阿纳姆丛林东北部雍古族玛塔(Yolŋu–Matha)混居群落的语言中,数百个词语确认是来自外来语望加锡语。例如,雍古族用作酒名的楠纳基,就是望加锡人传来的。这个词源自荷兰语中形容大茴香酒的词语。同样,望加锡外来语卢比亚

THE RESONANCE OF THE MACASSANS AND THE TREPANG TRADE IN ABORIGINAL CULTURAL TRADITIONS TODAY

Perhaps, one day, more than 200 years ago, during the short lulls in the wet season when the sea becomes still and reflects the giant triangles of cloud on the horizon, Aboriginal men fishing from their canoes saw odd shapes on the horizon. They might have waited to see what these shapes were, travelling slowly, bobbing up and down on the waves and heading for land. Their first encounter may have been cautious and, if the visitors asked for fresh water, that may have been the beginning of a friendship. That was the story told in the opera entitled *Trepang* performed by the descendants of Aboriginal and Macassan people in their own languages, Macassarese and Gupapuyngu.[71] There was little sentimentality in the performance. It was a robust and humorous telling of the tensions of their first encounter with all the excitement and romance of such beginnings. On stage, the Macassans arrived with a cyclonic storm, desperate for fresh water. The first act was enriched with the stylised performances by Gupapuyngu men of the sudden drunkenness that resulted from their first bottle of *nganaji*, the Yolŋu word for the Dutch liquor, aniseed, brought by the Macassans. They also acted out the smoking of tobacco in long pipes and the martial arts duels. These recitals were entwined with the tale of 'a romantic "love trade" in which a Yolŋu girl meets a Macassan sailor, who trades with her parents for her hand'.[72] The Yolŋu songs performed in *Trepang* 'are full of sorrow, stories of abduction and the forced trade in Yolŋu women that developed in the Macassan period'.[73] As Lisa Palmer observed of this intercultural narrative, 'the Macassan goods brought both benefit and turmoil for the Yolŋu. Knives and alcohol proved lethal, especially when combined with angry retribution over the abductions of Yolŋu women.'[74] The opera also celebrated the Yolŋu–Macassan kinship ties. 'Mansjur, the male lead in the Macassan cast, is a grandson of a Macassan sea captain, Otching Daeng Rangka, who abducted and married the great-grandmother of Matjuwi, the senior Yolŋu ceremony leader in Trepang'.[75] This relationship was a highly regarded one, much honoured by Yolŋu people. Set in Arnhem Land, the opera was also 'a reminder of the past greatness of their Kingdom of Gowa and of the seafaring might that their port city, Macassar, once enjoyed, positioned at the centre of East Indies trade routes'.[76]

For many Aboriginal people, the time of the Macassans has left a pronounced cultural and historical legacy. For instance, Macassarese became the *lingua franca* of much of the north Australian coast. It was used not only in dealings with Macassan trepangers, but also between distant Aboriginal peoples whilst in the employment of the Macassans. In northeast Arnhem Land there are hundreds of identified Macassan loan words in the languages encompassed by the Yolŋu–Matha bloc. For example, *nganaji* is the Yolŋu term for alcohol inherited from the Macassans. It derives from the Dutch term for their aniseed liqueur. Likewise, the Macassan loan word 'ṟuppiya', derived from the Malay term 'rupiah', is still used in reference to present day Australian currency. This indicates that the concept of a currency precedes the introduction of the Australian cash economy to Arnhem Land. It also bears noting the great symbolic power of this specific concept of currency which incorporates the historical values dating from the Macassan period. There are many other linguistic and cultural references to the Macassan long presence on the northern coasts.[77]

Charlie Matjuwi
Burarrwanga
Moiety: Yirritja
Clan: Gumatj
Lul'wurriwuy Leaving Elcho Island
1994
Acrylic on bark
144 x 52cm
Elcho Island,
North East Arnhem Land
ABART-1178
Museum and Art Gallery of the Northern Territory

Charlie Matjuwi
Burarrwanga
部落分支：Yirritja
部落：Gumatj
Lul'wurriwuy离开埃尔科岛
1994年
树皮丙烯
144 x 52cm
阿纳姆丛林东北部埃尔科岛
ABART-1178
北领地博物馆和美术馆

1.

2.   3.

1. Larrtjanga
Moiety: Dhuwa
Clan: Ngaymil
No title
c.1980
Natural pigments
on stringy bark
(Eucalyptus tetradonta)
109.5 x 57.5 x 3.5cm
X97870
Museum Victoria

2. Mawalan Marika #1
Moiety: Dhuwa
Clan: Rirratjingu
No title
c.1960
Natural pigments
on stringy bark
(Eucalyptus tetradonta)
132 x 61.4 x 4.5cm
X81367
Museum Victoria

3. Gawirrin Gumana
Moiety: Yirritja
Clan: Dhaḻwangu
No title
c.1960
Natural pigments
on stringy bark
(Eucalyptus tetradonta)
51.5 x 10.9cm
X97860
Museum Victoria

1. Larrtjanga
部落分支: Dhuwa
部落: Ngaymil
无题
约1980年
树皮，天然色素 (四齿桉)
109.5 x 57.5 x 3.5cm
X97870
维多利亚州博物馆

2. Mawalan Marika #1
部落分支: Dhuwa
部落: Rirratjingu
无题
约1960年
树皮，天然色素 (四齿桉)
132 x 61.4 x 4.5cm
X81367
维多利亚州博物馆

3. Gawirrin Gumana
部落分支: Yirritja
部落: Dhaḻwangu
无题
约1960年
树皮，天然色素 (四齿桉)
51.5 x 10.9cm
X97860
维多利亚州博物馆

1.

1. Wonggu
Moiety: Dhuwa
Clan: Djapu
No title
c.1935
Natural pigments
on stringy bark
(Eucalyptus tetradonta)
67.5 x 57.8cm
Eastern Arnhem Land
(DT38)
The Donald Thomson
Collection,
the University of Melbourne
and Museum Victoria

2. Wonggu
Moiety: Dhuwa
Clan: Djapu
No title
c.1935
Natural pigments
on stringy bark
(Eucalyptus tetradonta)
46.3 x 65cm
Caledon Bay,
Eastern Arnhem Land
(DT 30)
The Donald Thomson
Collection,
the University of Melbourne
and Museum Victoria

3. Wuluwirr
Moiety: Dhuwa
Clan: Djapu
No title
c.1935
Natural pigments
on stringy bark
(Eucalyptus tetradonta)
52 x 64.8cm
Caledon Bay,
Eastern Arnhem Land
(DT 31)
The Donald Thomson
Collection,
the University of Melbourne
and Museum Victoria

1. Wonggu
部落分支：Dhuwa
部落：Djapu
无题
约1935年
树皮，天然色素（四齿桉）
67.5 x 57.8cm
阿纳姆丛林东部 (DT38)
墨尔本大学和维多利亚州博物馆Donald Thomson藏品

2. Wonggu
部落分支：Dhuwa
部落：Djapu
无题
约1935年
树皮，天然色素（四齿桉）
46.3 x 65cm
阿纳姆丛林东部Caledon湾 (DT 30) 墨尔本大学和维多利亚州博物馆Donald Thomson藏品

3. Wuluwirr
部落分支：Dhuwa
部落：Djapu
无题
约1935年
树皮，天然色素（四齿桉）
52 x 64.8cm
阿纳姆丛林东部Caledon湾 (DT 31) 墨尔本大学和维多利亚州博物馆Donald Thomson藏品

2.

3.

53

(ruppiya)源自马来语卢比(rupiah)，这个词目前仍用来指代现行的澳大利亚货币。这表明，货币概念进入阿纳姆丛林的时间要早于澳大利亚现金交易经济。它也充分体现了这种蕴藏着望加锡时代历史价值的特定货币概念的巨大象征意义。此外，还有很多其他语言和文化能够证明望加锡人在北部海岸的长期生活印迹。[77]

随着与望加锡人商品交易及全面文化接触的发展，土著区域文化和宇宙观也开始发生变化、创新、瓦解并最终彻底改观。

海岸地区土著人复杂的口叙历史、歌曲套曲、祭祀舞蹈和艺术作品里，保留着对这些物质和文化交流的详细记述[78]。对交流时期的口述和记载，描绘了土著部落与来客之间具有社会和贸易关系特点的交流互动。这些交流，形成了对土著海岸部落财产权利不同程度的认可，以及与部落及个人所确立的不同程度的贸易协议体系。若一方认为这些权利和协议受到侵犯，那么就会引发分歧，从而不可避免地发生冲突。

虽然望加锡人带来交易的商品，给土著海岸部落带来了重大物质利益及一段加快文化创新的时期，但很多商品也成了社会骚乱的根节。尽管存在冲突，但望加锡人的影响力仍然遍及阿纳姆丛林社会，这一点在宗教象征和贸易对象等意思上更为重要[79]。

在葬礼和成人礼等宗教仪式中，土著人会举办古代先祖们所举办的活动。这些历史叙述，象征意义丰富，有时只是含蓄表达了深层意思。我们可以在叙事歌曲、身体装饰物的复杂设计及宗教仪式用品和神圣的艺术设计中探寻到土著文化隐含的价值和微妙含义的蛛丝马迹。对雍古族人来说，语言具有力量，尤其是玛尼凯(manikay)诗里所使用的深奥语言。仪式中最引人注目的当属表演者的个人表现、投入和服装，他们用力拍打沙土，蹦蹦跳跳，踢起一股股白沙，以庄重深情而且经常又带着狂欢的方式来召唤着祖先。

在将死者的灵魂送往另一个世界的安葬传统中，也有他们与望加锡远航船员关系密切的内容。人们在沙滩上画出望加锡人的敞舱船(perahu)，当作是将运送死者灵魂的工具。孔洞是一些空木棺的神圣设计之一，而敞舱船(perahu)则象征着灵魂赖以逃脱至另一个世界的通道。

With the trading of goods and intensive cultural contact with the Macassans came change, innovation, disruption and eventual adaptation of regional Aboriginal culture and cosmology.

Detailed records of this material and cultural exchange remain in complex oral histories, song cycles, ceremonial dance and artistic works of the Aboriginal people of the coastal region.[78] The oral and written accounts of contact times portray the interactions between the Aboriginal groups and the visitors as characterised by social and trading relationships. These were underpinned to varying degrees by an acknowledgement of the property rights of coastal Aboriginal groups and by a system of trading protocols established with groups as well as individuals. In cases where these rights and protocols were believed by either party to be infringed, dispute and, inevitably, conflict was incited.

Whilst the goods that the Macassans brought and traded provided coastal Aboriginal groups with substantial material benefits and a period of heightened cultural innovation, many of these goods were also a cause of social turmoil. Despite the conflicts, Macassan influence abounds in Arnhem Land societies, and this is particularly important in the meaning of things, such as ritual emblems and trade objects.[79]

At religious ceremonies, such as funeral and initiation ceremonies, Aboriginal people celebrate events that took place in the sacred ancestral past. The narratives are rich with symbolism and the deeper meanings are, sometimes, only implied. Hints of the Aboriginal culture's hidden values and elaborate meanings are to be found in the song narratives, intricate designs of body decorations and religious paraphernalia of the ceremonies and sacred designs of the art. For the Yolŋu, words have power, especially the esoteric words used in the lyrics of their *manikay*. Most striking at the ceremonies is the personal effort, commitment and investment of the performers who pound the sand and leap up, kicking up fine streams of white dust, calling up the ancestors with great reverence, gust and, often, hilarity.

Among mortuary traditions, to send the spirits of the deceased to the other world, there is one that concerns their relationship with the Macassan seafarers. The *perahu* of the Macassans is represented sculpturally on sand beaches as a vehicle for the soul of the deceased. In some hollow log coffins, a bunghole is a part of the sacred design and the *perahu* represents the aperture through which the soul escapes to the other world.

These *larrkitj*, as these hollow log coffins are called by the moiety concerned, have been created by the artists and carvers of the Gumatj clan of northeast Arnhem Land for artistic and religious purposes for other ceremonies as well, such as the annual Garma Festival of Dance and Culture hosted by the Yothu Yindi Foundation on behalf of the clans. The Gumatj clan was one of several that welcomed the Macassans and found a place for them in their society. The celebration of the transformative ancestral Aboriginal figure Ganbulabula and of the equally influential Macassan history have a millenarian quality. This is an elaboration of the stated Yolŋu regard for their Macassan brothers, whose visits predated the coming of the British. More importantly, contact with the Macassans was characterised by

1. R.M. Berndt
Flag Dance 21 April 1964
Yirrkala
Courtesy of the University of Western Australia Berndt Museum of Anthropology
P18700

2. R.M. Berndt
Men performing the 'handkerchief dance', in the Jiridja [sic] *moiety mortuary sequence* 1 April 1964
The flags are symbols of farewell to the deceased's spirit, and one bears an anchor design; these relate to the 'Macassan' song cycle.
Yirrkala
Courtesy of the University of Western Australia Berndt Museum of Anthropology
P32648

1. R.M. Bernd
旗舞 1964年4月21日
Yirrkala
西澳大学Berndt提供
人类学博物馆
P18700

2. R.M. Berndt
Jiridja部落分支葬礼系列中，男人表演'手帕舞'
1964年4月1日
旗帜象征告别逝者魂灵，其中一面旗帜画有锚图；该图与望加锡套曲有关。
Yirrkala
西澳大学Berndt提供
人类学博物馆
P32648

这些拉科提(larrkitj)(所涉及土著分支对这种空木棺的叫法)由阿纳姆丛林东北部古玛提(Gumatj)部落的艺术家和雕刻家们制作，它们也会用于其他仪式的艺术和宗教用途，如尤荼·印迪基金会(Yothu Yindi Foundation)代表部落每年举办的嘎玛舞蹈文化节 (Garma Festival of Dance and Culture)。古玛提部落是几个欢迎望加锡人的部落之一，他们在自己的社会中给望加锡人腾出了容身之所。对富有变革能力的土著先祖人物甘布拉布拉(Ganbulabula)的崇拜以及对同样影响深远的望加锡历史的膜拜，都有一种千禧年的韵味在其中。这明确体现了雍古族人对这些远在英国人之前就到达此地的望加锡兄弟的重视。更重要的是，基于对土著人治理马瑞格及土著传统和权威的尊重，与望加锡人的交易往来基本体现了平等关系。这个地区的雍古族人采用安放石头方式来讲述望加锡人的故事，几十年来一直都不为传教士和政府所知。到20世纪90年代，雍古族人最终寻求对此的保护，直至今日，这已经成为深受重视的重要历史遗迹。同样，古玛提也保护了望加锡时代在此加工海参的一个石制烹煮区。这个地方也同样受到高度重视。

与欧洲人进入该地区相比，望加锡人的贸易时代被视为是一段建立在平等基础上的协商关系。与望加锡人交往过的澳大利亚北海岸土著人从这段重要历史时期中推断，其祖先以前曾参与过国际商业活动。这个推论有力的驳斥了那些认为土著人生活孤僻呆板、让人憎恶的说法。望加锡人尊重当地财产和土地权利的理念，其所带来的经济关系丰富了所有人的文化和物质生活。周小平用一捆捆涂成赭色的海参安装成的中国杆秤，也指出了这种关系的精神。这段历史交流的新旧文化符号，都散发着家庭和友谊无法衡量的价值。

1.

2.

relationships of equality involving exchange based —in the main— on respect for Aboriginal governance of Marege and for Aboriginal tradition and authority. The Yolŋu in this area created a stone arrangement telling the story of the Macassans and kept it secret from the missionaries and the Government for decades. Eventually, in the 1990s, Yolŋu sought protection for it and, today, it is a highly regarded site of historical significance. As well, the Gumatj clan protects a stone cooking area where the trepang was processed dating from the time of the Macassan visits. This place is also regarded with great reverence.

In contrast to the entry of the Europeans into the region, the period of trade with the Macassans is regarded as one of negotiated relationships built on relationships of equality. The Aboriginal people of the northern Australian coastline who encountered the Macassans deduce from that important period of their past that their people were engaged in international commerce. This inference counters the much-resented accounts of Aboriginal life as isolated and static. The Macassans paid regard to local concepts of property and land title, and the economic relationship was enriching culturally and materially for all concerned. The spirit of this relationship is alluded to in Zhou's installation of Chinese weights and scales with the bundles of trepang painted with ochre. The incalculable value of family and friendship emanates throughout the old and new cultural symbols of this historical exchange.

1. Rev TT Webb
Ṉalapal miyalk thu manda balabalyun warraga at Macacssan Well, Milingimbi.
[Senior women grinding cycad nuts atop midden at Macassan Well, Milingimbi]
c.1930
Courtesy of the University of Sydney Archives with the permission of Dr Joseph Gumbula.

2. *Macassar influence: Grave Post and Dupuns.*
Warramirri mättä Arnhem Land.
Photograph by D.F. Thomson.
Courtesy of Mrs D.M. Thomson and Museum Victoria

1. Rev TT Webb 牧师
Ṉalapal miyalk thu manda balabalyun warraga at Macacssan Well, Milingimbi.
[老年妇女在Milingimbi望加锡井边磨苏铁坚果]
约1930年
悉尼档案馆提供，承蒙Joseph Gumbula博士允许使用。

2. 望加锡影响：墓柱和Dupuns，
Warramirri mättä
阿纳姆丛林。
摄影： D.F. Thomson，
D.M. Thomson夫人和维多利亚州博物馆提供

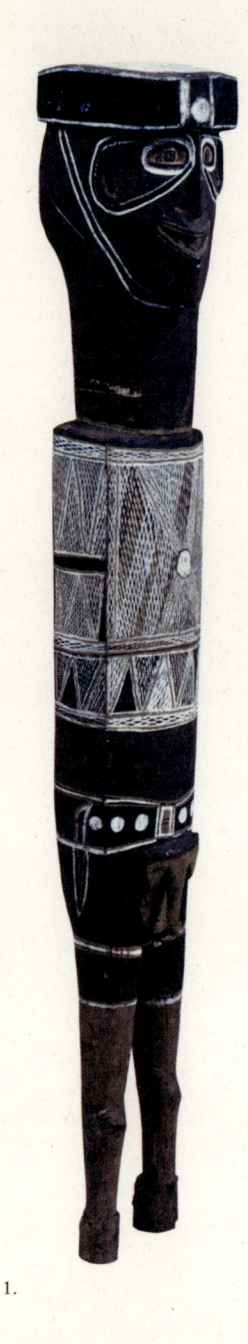

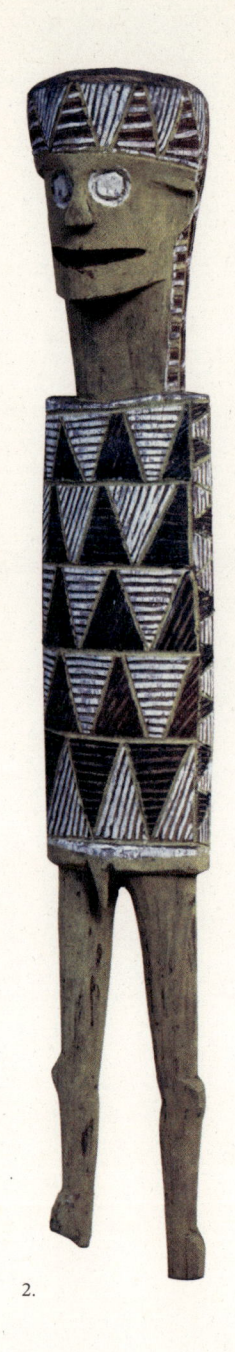

1. Maŋarawuy
Moiety: Yirritja
Clan: Gumatj
No title (Wurramu)
Date collected 1/1/1946
Wood, natural pigments
85 x 15cm
Courtesy of the University
of Western Australia Berndt
Museum of Anthropology
WU401

2. Maŋarawuy
Moiety: Yirritja
Clan: Gumatj
No title (Wurramu)
Date collected 1/1/1946
Wood, natural pigments
66 x 12.5cm
Courtesy of the University
of Western Australia Berndt
Museum of Anthropology
WU404

3. Margarwala
Moiety: Yirritja
Clan: Mandjigai
No title (Wurramu)
Date collected 1/1/1947
Wood, natural pigments
H125cm
Courtesy of the University
of Western Australia Berndt
Museum of Anthropology
WU438

4. Maŋarawuy
Moiety: Yirritja
Clan: Gumatj
No title (Wurramu)
Date collected 1/1/1946
Wood, natural pigments
59 x 11cm
Courtesy of the University
of Western Australia Berndt
Museum of Anthropology
WU412

5. Wananjambi and
Mambur (or Mick Marambur)
Moiety: Yirritja
Clan: Unconfirmed
No title (Wurramu)
Date collected 1/1/1961
Wood, natural pigments
H68.5cm
Courtesy of the University
of Western Australia Berndt
Museum of Anthropology
WU931

4.   5.

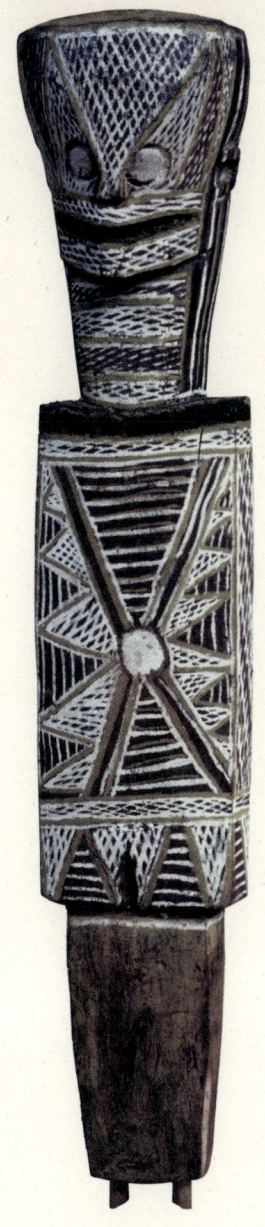

1. Maŋarawuy
部落分支: Yirritja
部落: Gumatj
无题 (Wurramu)
收藏日期: 1946年1月1日
木质，天然色素
85 x 15cm
西澳大学Berndt提供
人类学博物馆
WU401

2. Maŋarawuy
部落分支: Yirritja
部落: Gumatj
无题 (Wurramu)
收藏日期: 1946年1月1日
木质，天然色素
66 x 12.5cm
西澳大学Berndt提供 人类学博物馆
WU404

3. Margarwala
部落分支: Yirritja
部落: Mandjigai
无题 (Wurramu)
收藏日期: 1947年1月1日
木质，天然色素
H125cm
西澳大学Berndt提供
人类学博物馆
WU438

4. Maŋarawuy
部落分支: Yirritja
部落: Gumatj
无题 (Wurramu)
收藏日期: 1946年1月1日
木质，天然色素
59 x 11cm
西澳大学Berndt提供
人类学博物馆
WU412

5. Wananjambi和Mambur
(或Mick Marambur)
部落分支: Yirritja
部落: 未确定
无题 (Wurramu)
收藏日期: 1941年1月1日
木质，天然色素
H68.5cm
西澳大学Berndt提供
人类学博物馆
WU931

59

望加锡精神的复苏

2005年，祖先们曾于一百多年前到过阿纳姆丛林的望加锡塔宾·斯瓦丽亚(Takbing Siwaliya)演员们参加了嘎玛节。男人们用声音、芦笛和击鼓来表演音乐剧，女人们则戴着面纱翩翩起舞。与来过马瑞格的祖先一样，他们也受到印度尼西亚伊斯兰文化的约束，只能表演望加锡特色的传统音乐剧。彼得·唐纳(Peter Toner)剖析了玛尼凯流派的雍古族歌曲，他在翻译歌词后发现，与望加锡人的关系在雍古族音乐传统里的重要地位[80]。至少在一套雍古族套曲中能够清晰辨别出阿拉伯古典宗教音乐的曲调。唐纳解释说，雍古族歌手即兴创作了神圣的词句，但祖先和人类的历史却成了当代表演的范本和模板[81]。唐纳说，船、锚、剑、旗"都是最重要的符号之一"[82]。详细分析歌曲主题后，唐纳认识到，格入如(garurru)指的是旗帜，象征着"一位名叫毕林尼吉(Birrinydji)的古代剑客，他开创了方方面面的达尔王古(Dhalwaŋu)文化，通常认为这段文化就是由于与望加锡人的交往而兴起的"[83]。布龙·布龙的一幅树皮画中也可明显看到桨和剑：我们可以看到海参的加工过程，男人、刀剑、船桨和冒着轻烟的棚屋；人物的繁多描绘了海参季节期间繁忙的工作。

对达尔王古人和其他涉及这段宇宙观的雍古族人而言，旗帜都尤为重要。旗帜高高地飘扬在船桅上，这条船环航阿纳姆丛林，从楠布瓦(Numbulwar)出发，沿途停靠在很多不同部落的祖籍地，随后往南穿过古如木入(Gurrumuru)河，并在古如木入锚定停靠。

......旗帜......成为祖先们在船上和古如木入从事活动的共同象征[84]。

. 自己，例如，古玛提部落使用黄旗，有时上面描绘着锚和锚索；瓦拉米力(Warramiri)部落使用纯白旗；楠迪力巴拉(Nundhirribala)使用较小的三角旗，旗面颜色丰富，但都有红色；而达尔王古(Dhalwangu)则选用红旗，有时会装饰着两把交叉剑和一个船锚。达尔王古人——和楠布瓦(Numbulwar)的楠迪力巴拉(Nundhirribala)人——有时会自称是"红旗族"，突出了旗帜所体现的共同身份。尽管证据错综复杂，但可以说旗帜是部落与各个敞舱船(perahu)船队关系的象征，甚至可能体现了他们最好滩头的港口地位[85]。2005年2月，雍古族长老当吉拉武伊·嘎啦维塔(Djangirrawuy Garawirrtja)为民族音乐学家

艾伦·科恩(Aaron Corn)列出了港口清单。每个港口(或称瓦加(wäŋa))都是雍古族的一个指定地方，每个地方也都有着一面旗帜(或称嘎力库(galiku))和一个特定的雍古族部落(或称玛拉(mala))：

1.

2.

REVIVING THE MACASSAN SPIRIT

In 2005, the Macassan performers of the ensemble Takbing Siwaliya, whose ancestors visited Arnhem Land over 100 years ago, attended the Garma Festival. The men performed extended musical works with voice, shawm and drums, while the women danced with veils. Like their ancestors who came to Marege, they are enjoined in the Islamic culture of Indonesia, but perform their distinctive Macassan musical traditions. Peter Toner analysed Yolŋu songs of the *manikay* genre and, by translating the song words, he revealed the importance of the relationship with the Macassans in these music traditions.[80] The melody of classical Arabic religious music can be discerned in at least one Yolŋu song cycle. Yolŋu singers improvise with sacred texts, Toner explained, but the ancestral and the human pasts are exemplars and templates for contemporary performance.[81] The ship, the anchor, the sword and the flag, as Toner noted, 'are among the most important symbols'.[82] After analysing the song subjects in detail, Toner realised that, *garurru* refers to the flag symbolising the 'ancestral figure called Birrinydji, the Swordsman, who instituted all aspects of the Dhaḻwaŋu clan culture, normally attributed to the historical period of Macassan contact'.[83] The paddle and the sword are evident in one of Bulunbulun's bark paintings: we can see the activity during the processing of the trepang, with men, swords, paddles and smoking huts; the density of the figures evoking the intense activity during the season.

The flag is a particularly important symbol not only for Dhalwangu people, and but also for other Yolŋu groups related through this body of cosmology. The flag was flown from the mast of a ship which sailed around the Arnhem Land coast from Numbulwar, stopping at the ancestral places of a number of different groups before sailing down the Gurrumuru River and dropping its anchor at Gurrumuru.

… The flag … establish[es] a homology between the ancestral activities on board the ship and those which took place at Gurrumuru.[84]

Every group that is involved has a distinctive flag which symbolises them: the Gumatj, for instance, use a yellow flag, which sometimes depicts an anchor and anchor cable; the Warramiri use a plain blue flag; the Nundhirribala use smaller, triangular flags with different colours, but always including red; and the Dhaḻwangu symbol is a red flag, sometimes adorned with two crossed swords and an anchor. Dhaḻwangu people sometimes refer to themselves —as well as the Nundhirribala from Numbulwar— as the 'red flag people', emphasising a shared identity based on the flag. Even though the evidence is complicated, it is possible to say that the flags are the emblems of clan relationships with the different fleets of *perahu* or, even perhaps, the status of their best beachheads as ports.[85] In February 2005 at Galiwin'ku, Yolŋu Elder Djaṉgirrawuy Garawirrtja listed the ports for ethnomusicologist Aaron Corn. Each port or *wäŋa* is a named place in the Yolŋu world, and each is associated with *galiku* or flag and a named Yolŋu group or *mala*:

1. Roy Pope
Aborigines, Melville Island
1941
nla.pic-an20354211-3
National Library of Australia

2. Chris Yawirryawirr
Moiety: Dhuwa
Clan: Balngarra
Dilly Bag
c.1988
Pandanus, multi-strand bush string handle, ochre, feather and cloth tassels
26 x 13.5 x 13.5cm
Eastern Arnhem Land
X90132
Museum Victoria

1. Roy Pope
土著人，梅尔维尔岛
1941年
nla.pic-an20354211-3
澳大利亚国立图书馆

2. Chris Yawirryawirr
部落分支：Dhuwa
部落：Balngarra
网袋
约1988年
露兜树，多股木线手把，赭石，羽毛和布穗
26 x 13.5 x 13.5cm
阿纳姆丛林东部
X90132
维多利亚州博物馆

Wäŋa (港口)	Galiku (旗帜)	Mala (部落)
Dholtji Manunu	黑色	Warramiri
Gurrumurudjiki	红色	Dhalwaŋu
Gamburriŋgadjiki	黄色	Gumatj
Minydharrŋura Wilirrŋura	绿色	Wangurri
Yarrinyyawuyŋu	白色	Munyuku Ŋurruwtthun
Djulkayaŋgi Bapadjambaŋ	蓝色	Birrkili
Baniyala Nikuniku Yilpara	蓝白相间	Madarrpa
Motatj	黑白相间	Wuymu Bäpayili Austronesian Whalers[86]

在甘特看来，望加锡人不仅仅是访客，"他们经常来到同一个地方，呆上几个月，有时住上一整年"[87]。他们"挖井造屋，给各个地方命名，有些地名也被雍古族所采纳"；他们"种了很多庄稼，其中包括罗望子"；他们"在国家和人民心中留下了历史烙印"[88]。地方的命名对望加锡人和雍古族人都具有同等重要意义。甘特总结说，"他们觉得自己已以某种方式宣布了对这片国土的所有权，他们对阿纳姆丛林一些渔民冠以的称呼邓*(daeng)*，成为当地人姓名的一个组成部分"[89]。同样，海岸线的旗帜象征以及几个世纪来由此经过的如此繁多的船舶、敞舱船*(perahu)*或欧洲帆船，也是这种关系的组成部分："雍古族认为，他们种植相思子*(abrus)*种子与欧洲人安插旗帜具有同等重要的象征意义"[90]。

Wäŋa (Port)	Galiku (Flag)	Mala (Group)
Dholtji Manunu	Black	Warramiri
Gurrumurudjiki	Red	Dhalwaŋu
Gamburriŋgadjiki	Yellow	Gumatj
Minydharrŋura Wilirrŋura	Green	Wangurri
Yarrinyyawuyŋu	White	Munyuku Ŋurruwtthun
Djulkayaŋgi Bapadjambaŋ	Blue	Birrkili
Baniyala Nikuniku Yilpara	Blue and White	Madarrpa
Motatj	Black and White	Wuymu Bäpayili Austronesian Whalers[86]

According to Ganter, the Macassans were more like settlers than visitors, 'coming regularly to the same places, staying for several months or sometimes a whole year'.[87] They 'dug wells and erected dwellings and named places, some of which became adopted by Yolŋu'; they 'planted a range of crops, including tamarind'; they 'left imprints on the country and the people'.[88] The significance of naming was as important for the Macassans as for Yolŋu. Ganter concluded that, '[t]hey felt they had some claim on the country: they bestowed the title of *daeng* on some of the sea people of Arnhem Land, which became part of local names'.[89] And again, the symbolism of flags along this coastline, together with so many craft, *perahu* or European sailing ships which had passed over the centuries, were part of the relationship: '[t]he Yolŋu understanding is that they planted *abrus* seed with the same symbolic significance as the Europeans planted flags'.[90]

纪念望加锡人

　　1988年，北领地博物馆和美术馆的彼得·斯佩利特 (Peter Spellit) 重新建造了一艘望加锡敞舱船 (perahu)，从澳大利亚出发前往苏拉威西，举行纪念航行。澳大利亚海事博物馆的杰里米·梅勒凡特 (Jeremy Mellefont) 说："船员们认为海洋是人民交流的纽带"。鉴于澳大利亚北部海域的丰富交通运输历史，英国人横跨重洋来到澳洲的历史，似乎也就没能给人留下太深的印象了[92]。

　　很多摇滚乐队也用歌声再现了望加锡人的故事。"1990年，米林金比·瓦林嘎乐队 (Milingimbi Wirrngga Band) 发行了一首名叫'塔科瑞纳 (Takkerena)'的歌曲，塔科瑞纳即当地海参加工营地的望加锡名称。3年后，曼宁瑞达 (Maningrida) 的日升乐队 (Sunrise Band) 以一首名叫兰巴纳·马尼·马尼 (Lembana Mani Mani) 为3JJJ电台取得巨大成功，而这也是望加锡人对该城镇的称呼"[93]。

　　尤茶·印迪 (Yothu Yindi) 乐队动听的"望加锡船员"合唱曲，则高度赞扬了望加锡人的勇敢精神。乐队2000年发行的最后一张专辑的主打歌《嘎玛》，歌词中弥漫着雍古族宗教的情绪或情感，给这段悲情的历史增添了一丝活泼情调。在歌词中，我们也能感受到望加锡人所带来之礼物的重要意义，以及其对雍古族人认识自身历史的持久影响：

　　与诸多此类纪念活动一样，布莱恩·嘎啦维塔 (Brian Garawirrtja) 的"望加锡印象"（包含在本目录里）也生动反应了阿纳姆丛林很多土著人对这段历史的深厚感情。

　　本次展览的很多元素也做到了这一点。

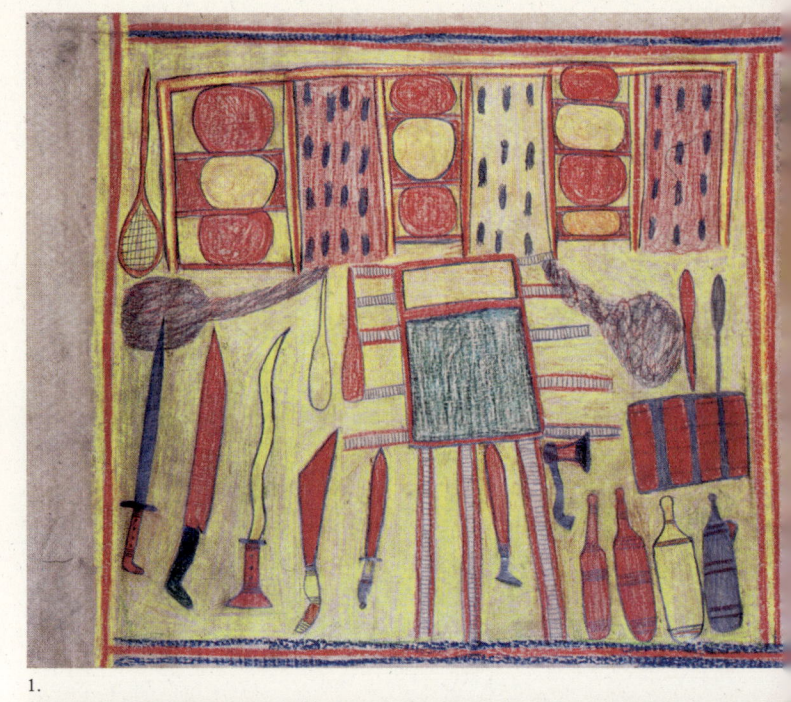

1.

2.

1. Mawalan Marika #1
Moiety: Dhuwa
Clan: Rirratjingu
No title.
Date collected 15/6/1947
Lumbar crayon
on butchers paper
61 x 71cm
Courtesy of the University
of Western Australia Berndt
Museum of Anthropology
WU7163

2. Mawalan Marika #1
Moiety: Dhuwa
Clan: Rirratjingu
No title.
Date collected 14/6/1947
Lumbar crayon
on butchers paper
61 x 153.5cm
Courtesy of the University
of Western Australia Berndt
Museum of Anthropology
WU7153

1. Mawalan Marika #1
部落分支：Dhuwa
部落：Rirratjingu
无题
收藏日期：15/6/1947
木材蜡笔，包肉纸
61 x 71cm
西澳大学Berndt提供
人类学博物馆
WU7163

2. Mawalan Marika #1
部落分支：Dhuwa
部落：Rirratjingu
无题
收藏日期：1947年6月14日
木材蜡笔，包肉纸
61 x 153.5cm
西澳大学Berndt提供
人类学博物馆
WU7153

COMMEMORATING THE MACASSANS

In 1988, Peter Spellit from the Museum and Art Gallery of the Northern Territory reconstructed a Macassan *perahu* for a commemorative journey from Australia to Sulawesi. According to Jeremy Mellefont of the Australian Maritime Museum: '[s]ailors see oceans as what connects people'.[91] Thinking about the rich history of traffic in Australia's northern seas, the British leap across to the antipodes begins to seem less impressive.[92]

Responses to the Macassan story have also come from a number of rock bands. 'In 1990, *Milingimbi Wirrngga Band* released a song called "Takkerena", which was the Macassan name for the trepanging camp in this area. Three years later, Maningrida's *Sunrise Band* produced a hit for 3JJJ titled *Tembana Mani Mani*, the Macassan name for their town'.[93]

In 'Macassan Crew' by Yothu Yindi, the bravery of the Macassans is honoured in the chorus of this beautiful ballad. Opening the band's final album, *Garma*, released in 2000, the emotional or affective register of Yolŋu religious references throughout this song's lyrics adds piquancy to its lamentation of the past. The references to the gifts of the Macassans and their abiding influence in Yolŋu perceptions of their history can also be sensed in the lyrics:

Like so many of these commemorative acts, Brian Garawirrtja's 'Macassan Reflections' —included in this catalogue— is a moving statement on the depth of feeling that many Aboriginal people of Arnhem Land feel for this history.

So too, do elements of this exhibition.

Yendharama birrapirra
Tradewinds blow
The southern cross
Taking their prau
Across the sea
They came in peace
Through the Ashmore Reef
Smoke and steel
And the Tamarind seed

Steer it up right
Steer it up true
Navigate the morning star
Brave Macassan crew

Sailed on through
The hole in the wall
The place we call Rarrakala
To the shores of the far North East
Smoke, steel and the Tamarind tree
Gapala Mangatjay
Gapala Gurrumulnga

Navigate the morning star
Brave Macassan crew

Miyaman Matjala,
Miyaman Gurrumulnga,
Daynggatjing Garrnhdalu,
Daymulung Wila'wila'yun,
Miyaman Mangatjay,
Miyaman Gurrumulngu
Daynggatjing Garrnhdalu,
Daymulung Wila'wila'yun,

Steer it up right
Steer it up true
Navigate the morning star
Brave Macassan crew

海参：展览

　　周小平和约翰·布龙·布龙的艺术作品，体现了两名杰出艺术家独特新颖的跨文化合作模式。他们一同阐释了自己与这些历史事件的关系。他们的作品将艺术家们放在过去和现在的景致中，尤其是周小平，他以浓厚的笔墨画了一幅布龙·布龙站立在独特灌木丛中的肖像。这幅画利用古代传统方式，叙述了这里曾经出现过的先辈和地方。除了通过艺术、表演和歌曲形式，土著文化里还能以何种形式来传承历史？周小平对布龙·布龙与"望加锡时代"人际和家谱关系的阐述，也遵循着这个传统。周小平的中国鲤鱼，变成了布龙·布龙海水国度里的神鱼。雕刻着精美蓝色图形的饭碗，漂浮在这片连接着中国大陆、中国南海群岛及马瑞格的海面上。在他们共同创作的作品里，周小平丰富、有时又生动活泼的颜色和中国视觉语言，与土著交叉阴影及图形元素的古典形式设计形成了优美的对比，描绘了望加锡人及与之和睦相处的雍古族人等先辈形象。周小平曾在阿纳姆丛林与雍古族人一同生活，他有一幅作品描绘了一个男人正从海上靠岸，远处的人们正举旗跳舞，生动地表达了他对雍古族人与海之间亲密情感的认识。

　　周小平和布龙·布龙采用特殊方式描绘了将其祖先连接在一起的海洋和贸易航线，其尊重历史及古代男女的独特视角构成了这次展览的基调，以艺术品和物品生动反应了古代人的探险之旅。

　　本次展览也将出现其他艺术家的作品：拉普伦·达玛兰吉（Lapulung Dhamarrandji）创作了令人惊叹的望加锡祖先瓦拉姆·马拉·博吉利（Warramu Mala-Birrkili）的雕像。还有一些如创作了格鲁特岛（Groote Eylandt）岩石艺术的古代不知姓名艺术家。此外还有一些纸上作品。这些丰富的艺术形式与博物馆的物品一同再现了"望加锡时代"的记忆。

　　本次展览的很多早期树皮画、澳大利亚北海岸海参贸易从业者的望加锡制品以及历史档案图片，都是向澳大利亚顶级收藏机构借来的，其中包括北领地博物馆和美术馆、维多利亚博物馆、北领地图书馆、南澳大利亚州州立图书馆、南澳大利亚州美术馆、澳大利亚国家档案局以及澳大利亚国家博物馆。树皮画的收藏历史非常有趣，这涉及到人类学家罗纳德（Ronald）和凯瑟琳·伯恩特（Catherine Berndt）、探险家以及藏品丰富的收藏家。

TREPANG: THE EXHIBITION

The artworks by Zhou Xiaoping and John Bulunbulun represent an original and innovative cross-cultural collaboration between two accomplished artists. They have come together to depict their own relationships with these historical events. Their paintings place the artists in the landscape, both past and present, especially in Zhou's strong portrait of Bulunbulun standing in the distinctive savannah landscape. It draws on ancient tradition to interpret the presence of the ancestral in the person and the place. How could history be preserved in Aboriginal culture except through art, performance and song? Zhou's interpretation of Bulunbulun's personal and genealogical link to the 'Macassan time' follows this tradition. The Koi fish of Zhou's China transforms into the sacred fish of Bulunbulun's saltwater country. Rice bowls with delicate blue patterns float on the sea that joins China, the archipelago of the 'South Seas' and Marege. In their joint works, Zhou's rich, sometimes vibrant colours and Chinese visual language contrast beautifully with the classical Aboriginal formal designs of the cross-hatching and figurative elements depicting ancestral beings, such as Macassans and the Yolŋu men who befriended them. Zhou has lived in Arnhem Land with Yolŋu people and his understanding of their intimacy with the sea is expressed in the image of a man pulling the sea into shore while men with flags dance beyond.

The distinctive ways in which Zhou and Bulunbulun represent the sea and the trade route that linked their ancestors anchor this exhibition with a unique vision that honours the past and the men and women of long ago, whose adventures are intimated in these artworks and objects.

Other artists are represented here too: Lapulung Dhamarrandji has produced a startling sculpture of a Macassan ancestor, Warramu Mala-Birrkili. Other artists are ancestral and unnamed, such as the painters who created the Groote Eylandt rock art. There are also works on paper such as that by the great Mawalan Marika I. This diversity of art forms combined with the museum objects give form to the memory of the 'Macassan time.'

A number of early bark paintings, Macassan and Chinese artefacts from the trepang trade encounters on Australia's northern shores and images from the historical records presented in this exhibition have been borrowed from Australia's finest collecting institutions including the Museum and Art Gallery of the Northern Territory, Museum Victoria, the Northern Territory Library, the State Library of South Australia, Art Gallery of South Australia, National Archives of Australia and the National Library of Australia. The history of collecting bark paintings is a fascinating one, involving anthropologists Ronald and Catherine Berndt, as well as, adventurers and wealthy art collectors.[94]

Lapulung Dhamarrandji
Moiety: Dhuwa
Clan: Djamparrpuyngu
Wurramu Mala-Birrkili
2007
Natural pigments on wood
225 x 120 x 120cm

Lapulung Dhamarrandji
部落分支: Dhuwa
部落: Djamparrpuyngu
Wurramu Mala-Birrkili
2007
木质，天然色素
225 x 120 x 120cm

这些树皮画是在这片土著土地上，陌生人（或称嗄皮吉(ngapiki)）人数尚不多时收集到的。基督传教士抵达前英国人在定居点的几次未遂企图，反而体现了土著人与望加锡人的关系取得了巨大的成功。这种关系延续了两个世纪，远远长于白种人在澳大利亚北部的定居时间。

大约在1910年左右，在海参贸易"几乎绝迹"时[95]，雍古族人可能还在观察着雨季初期的地平线，等待着故事中敞舱船(perahu)船队乘着季风出现的景象。那时，英国占领者已终结这段漫长的关系。第二年，只有两条船和8名牌照持有人从事这个产业。由于弗雷德·格雷(Fred Gray)等人还在与土著工人从事海参贸易，海参捕捞业仍在继续，但只是因为还有土著人在从事捕捞工作。乔治·荷博·桑特(George Herber Sunter)等一些海参捕捞者也有着自己的冒险故事[96]，但他们所从事的都不是雍古族记忆中"望加锡时代"的工作，也没有《海参》艺术家们所表达的那种浪漫主义情怀。

这项贸易突然中止，但"望加锡时代"的影响以及望加锡人终止每年来此一次所带来的失落感，仍然萦绕在土著人的心中。本次展览中，周小平的作品里就描绘了土著人看到地平线出现望加锡敞舱船(perahu)时所表现出来的愉快心情。美冠鹦鹉和纸牌，代表着人们的愉悦和激动，以及远眺地平线时的满腔期待。

牢记这段融入传统、名称、岩画艺术、歌曲、宗教艺术的历史有如此之多的方式，无怪乎每一代人都能创造出"望加锡时代"新的纪念方式以及对这一时代做出丰富的社会、文化和物质创新。若"望加锡时代"象征着过去那段冒险而精彩的岁月，那么它也代表着新的改造时期，以及对友谊活跃人类生活的期盼。

1.

2.

3.

4.

These bark paintings were collected when there were only a few *ngapiki*, or strangers, in this Aboriginal domain. The few unsuccessful attempts at settlement by the British, before the Christian missionaries arrived, show just how successful the Aboriginal–Macassan relationship was. The latter lasted for two centuries, longer than white settlement in north Australia.

In or around 1910, when trepanging had been 'almost entirely abandoned',[95] Yolŋu people might have watched the early wet season horizon, waiting for the tell tale signs of *perahu* fleets on the monsoon wind. By then, British dominion had ended the long relationship. In the following year only two boats and eight licence holders were engaged in the industry. With men like Fred Gray trepanging with Aboriginal workers, the trepang fishery continued, but only because Aboriginal people worked the fishery. There were other trepangers like George Herbert Sunter with his adventure tales,[96] but none as engaging as the Yolŋu memories of the 'Macassan time' nor as romantic as the artists of *Trepang*.

The trade was halted suddenly, but the impact of the 'Macassan time' and the sense of loss with the ending of their annual visits commemorated still. In this exhibition, the sense of joy that must have been felt as their *perahu* were sighted on the horizon is portrayed in Zhou's work. A cockatoo and playing cards signal the pleasure and excitement and people watching the horizon, the expectancy.

With so many ways to remember this history embedded in traditions, names, rock art, songs and sacred art, it should not be surprising that new ways of commemorating the 'Macassan time' and the rich social, cultural and material innovations of this time are created with each generation. If the 'Macassan time' symbolises the past, an adventurous and exciting age, it also represents the new and transformative, and a vision of the potential for friendship to enliven human affairs.

1. Ted Ryko *Trepang hunters, Croker Island, N.T* Shows group of Aboriginal women and child. 1916 Croker Island. Ted Ryko Collection PH0055/0018 Northern Territory Library

2. Photographer unknown *Trepang Camp* Fred Gray's trepang camp, Caledon Bay, c.1934. Caledon Bay Peace Mission Collection PH0731/0057 Northern Territory Library

3. Photographer unknown *Drying Trepang* Fred Gray and an Aboriginal man with drying trepang, c.1934 Caledon Bay Peace Mission Collection PH0731/0062 Northern Territory Library

4. Photographer unknown *Treating Trepang* Aboriginals treating trepang at Fred Gray's camp, c.1934. Caledon Bay Peace Mission Collection PH0731/0053 Northern Territory Library

1. Ted Ryko 海参捕捞者
北领地Croker岛
描绘一群土著妇女儿童
1916年
Croker岛。Ted Ryko藏品
PH0055/0018
北领地图书馆

2. 摄影：未知
海参营
Caledon湾Fred Gray海参营
约1934年
Caledon湾,
和平队藏品 PH0731/0057
北领地图书馆

3. 摄影：未知
晒干海参
Fred Gray和土著男子晒
干海参
约1934年
Caledon Bay,
和平队藏品 PH0731/0062
北领地图书馆

4. 摄影：未知
加工海参
土著人在Fred Gray营地加
工海参
约1934年
Caledon Bay,
和平队藏品 PH0731/0053
北领地图书馆

END NOTES

1. I am indebted to Lisa Palmer and Odette Mazel, who have previously written about the Macassan relationships with Yolŋu, for permission to use material from our earlier publications (see Marcia Langton, Odette Mazel and Lisa Palmer, 'The "Spirit" of the Thing: The Boundaries of Aboriginal Economic Relations at Australian Common Law' (2006) 17 *Australian Journal of Anthropology* 307). I am also indebted to the Bundanon Trust for their generous support in providing a retreat to write this essay. Several people helped with research, editorial advice and helpful discussions of historical dilemmas and I must acknowledge them and express my gratitude: Julian Cleary, Zoe Scanlon, Jelmer Procee, Kartia Snoek and Sarah Morris.

2. John Cawte, *Healers of Arnhem Land* (2001, University of New South Wales Press) 68.

3. Alison Mercieca, curator of the National Museum of Australia, in her discussion of an exhibition of Macassan objects, observed that there is some dispute among Australian historians about the historical and archaeological evidence for the earliest date of Macassan arrival in Australia and whether they came annually. She said:

The precise year of the first voyage is not known from the historical or archaeological records. The consensus among historians and archaeologists has been to place the date of the first voyage in the first half of the eighteenth century. Whether or not the voyages were made annually at this point is uncertain. However recent studies of trepang imports and exports to and from Makassar suggest that in the 1720s the trepang industry was still in its infancy, and as the century went by the industry intensified. So fishermen were sailing further and further afield to collect the trepang to supply the demand.

A recent study by Campbell Macknight reconsiders a date of about 1780, formally dismissed by scholars. This date is based on the record of Matthew Flinders who encountered Macassan fishermen in 1803 … In any case I think we can say that by 1780 there was certainly a trepang industry in Australian waters and that by this time annual voyages were being organised from Makassar to the Arnhem Land coast to fish for trepang:

Alison Mercieca, 'From Makassar to Marege' to the Museum: Trepang Processing Industry in Arnhem Land', National Museum of Australia, *Behind the Scenes: Australian Journeys series,* 7 July 2008, http://www.nma.gov.au/audio/transcripts/NMA_Mercieca_20080709.html at 5 March 2010.

4. The slug is called trepang in Australia, South-East Asia and the Pacific, and also *bêche-de-mer,* a French term derivative of the Portuguese *bicho-do-mar.* It is also called the sea cucumber. This marine animal is an echinoderm. 'The class *Holothuroidea* contains more than 1000 species … which live predominantly in tropical waters such as those to the north of Australia. Their lengths range from 10 to 50 centimetres but sometimes they can grow up to more than a metre. They also range in colour including black, white, grey, brown, blue and red': *ibid.* The species inhabits the sandy floor of the coastal littoral regions and reef flats.

5. The spelling of Macassan in this essay follows Charles Campbell Macknight rather than modern spellings because of the heavy reliance on Macknight's published works and on other historians who similarly use this spelling.

6. The most definitive work is that of Charles Campbell Macknight, *The Voyage to Marege', Macassan Trepangers in Northern Australia* (1976, Melbourne University Press). See also John Cawte, *Healers of Arnhem Land,* 69.

7. Pin-tsun Chang, 'The Rise of Chinese Mercantile Power in VOC Dutch East Indies' (2009) 3 *Chinese Southern Diaspora Studies* 3, 5–10.

8. *ibid* 10.

9. *ibid.*

10. *ibid.*

11. *ibid.*

12. *ibid.* Chang's account is very thorough. He writes: 'The Dutch United East India Company was established in 1602, annulled and nationalized in 1795. As its charter remained in force until 31 December 1799, the VOC formally came to an end at the turn of the century. From 1800 to 1949, when the Republic of Indonesia officially came into being, for one and a half centuries the East Indies was ruled as a colony by the Dutch, constituting the colonial period of the archipelagos': at 3.

13. *ibid* 7.

14. *ibid.*

15. Hans W Y Yeung, 'Macau (Macao): Long-Lasting Colonial Outpost' in Keat Gin Ooi (ed), *Southeast Asia: A Historical Encyclopedia from Angkor Wat to East Timor Volume 3* (2004, ABC-CLIO) 810, 810. According to Yeung, this was a stratagem on the part of the Chinese administration keen to prevent piracy. China retained sovereignty and Chinese residents were subject to Chinese law, but the territory was under Portuguese administration.

16. *ibid.* There were three major routes linking China to a global market which the Portuguese plied after they obtained their monopoly at Macao for a rent: 'Macau-Melaka-Goa-Lisbon, Guangzhou (Canton)-Macau-Nagasaki and Macau-Manila-Mexico': at 810.

17. *ibid.*

18. I use the historical, or pre-independence spelling of this port, Macassar, to be consistent with the period under discussion here. On maps today, it is spelt Makassar in accordance with the official language of the Republic of Indonesia, Bahasa Indonesia. The Celebes is now Sulawesi.

19. Chang, 'The Rise of Chinese Mercantile Power', 13.

20. *ibid* 10. Chang also observes that 'in the later half of the eighteenth century several tax farming tycoons emerged in central and eastern Java, nearly all of them coming from these two clans. These Chinese families were also closely tied by intermarriage [and] their cooperation was so successful that they monopolized most tax farming business in those regions': at 13.

21. Madeleine Zelin, 'Book Review: The Canton Trade, Life and Enterprise on the China Coast, 1700–1845' (2007) 81(1) *Business History Review* 207, 207.

22. Paul A Van Dyke, *The Canton Trade: Life and Enterprise on the China Coast, 1700–1845* (2005, Hong Kong University Press) 178–9.

23. Hans Konrad Van Tilburg, 'Book Review: Gang Deng, Chinese Maritime Activities And Socioeconomic Development, C. 2100 B.C.–1900 A.D.' (1999) 10(1) *Journal of World History* 213, 214.

24. Australian National Maritime Museum exhibition (1997), cited in Peter Lister, Didjeridu & Traditional Music of the Top End: Makassans http://www.manikay.com/didjeridu/macass.shtml at 5 March 2010.

25. *Yarmirr v Northern Territory (2)* (1998) 82 FCR 533, 558 (Olney J).

26. *ibid.*

27. *ibid.*

28. Miriam Estensen, *The Life of Matthew Flinders* (2002, Crows Nest: Allen & Unwin) 264.

29. *ibid* 266.

30. Matthew Flinders, *A Voyage to Terra Australis Volume 2* (1814, Pall Mall: G & W Nicol) 231.

31. *ibid* 230.

32. Estensen, *The Life of Matthew Flinders,* 266.

33. Flinders, *A Voyage to Terra Australis Volume 2,* 232.

34. Estensen, *The Life of Matthew Flinders,* 266.

35. *ibid.*

36. *ibid.*

37. Flinders, *A Voyage to Terra Australis Volume 2,* 231.

38. Rachel Ganter, 'Turning the Map Upside Down' (2005) 9 *Griffith Review* 167, 169–70.

39. *ibid.*

40. Barker also served at King George's Sound in Western Australia. He was speared to death by three Ngerrinjerri men near the mouth of the Murray River on 30th April 1831. He gave his name to Mount Barker township, region and mountain, on the southeastern outskirts of the Mount Lofty ranges.

41. The Dessert Star, 'In Search for Collet Barker' (29 November 2007) http://www.desertdreams.com.au/iblog/C1759100478/E20071129143436/index.html at 6 March 2010.

42. *ibid.*

43. Collet Barker, Derek John Mulvaney, Neville Green, *Commandant of Solitude: The Journals of Captain Collet Barker, 1828-1831* (1992, Melbourne University Press) 273.

44. *Yarmir v Northern Territory (2)* (1998) 82 FCR 533, 559.

45. Charles Campbell Macknight, 'Using Daeng Rangka (1845? - 1927)' in Bede Nairn (ed), *Australian Dictionary of Biography Volume 6* (1976, Melbourne University Press) 322–3.

46. *ibid.*

47. *ibid.*

48. *ibid.*

49. *ibid.*

50. *ibid.*

51. *ibid.*

52. *ibid.*

53. Charles Campbell Macknight, *The Macassans: A Study of the Early Trepang Industry along the Northern Territory Coast* (1969, PhD. Australian National University) 180. Macknight refers to Daeng Sarro as '"Suppu" Daeng Sarro, Professor Cense's informant, [who] was the son of Using Daeng Rangka's sister (and thus Mangngellai's cousin)': at 33.

54. *ibid* 182.

55. *ibid* 180.

56. Macknight, *The Macassans*, 180. Note that the villages of Renggang and Dompu, mentioned in Sarro's account, are both the names of suburbs of Macassar, Kampong Renggang and Kampong Dompu. The people of Kampong Dompu originally came from Dompu in Sumbawa. There is still an Aboriginal camp in Gray's Bay called Camburinga.

57. Scott Mitchell, 'A Transient Heritage: Trepanging Sites on the Cobourg Peninsula' (1995) 11 (2-3) *Historic Environment* 37, 38.

58. *ibid.*

59. Scott Mitchell, *Culture Contact and Indigenous Economies on the Cobourg Peninsula, Northwestern Arnhem Land* (1994, PhD. Thesis, Northern Territory University) 40.

60. Macknight *The Macassans: A Study of the Early Trepang Industry along the Northern Territory Coast* (1969, PhD. Australian National University) Ch 13, 405.

61. *ibid.*

62. *ibid* 441.

63. *ibid* 450.

64. *ibid*

65. Brad Smith, 'Mobile Traders or Impoverished Harvesters: A re-evaluation of eastern-wares from 'Macassan" trepanging sites in northern Australia' (1999, Thesis Abstract) http://www.une.edu.au/humanities/archpal/theses.php at 5 March 2010.

66. Cawte, *Healers of Arnhem Land*, 68.

67. Ian Keen, *Aboriginal Economy and Society: Australia at the Threshold of Colonisation* (2003, Oxford University Press) 100, 366–7 citing William Lloyd Warner, *A Black Civilization: A Social Study of an Australian Tribe* (1st ed, 1937).

68. Ganter, 'Turning the Map Upside Down', 171.

69. *ibid.*

70. *ibid.* Ganter describes the circumstances which led to her possession of this map: 'The map was photographed by Batchelor College students and published in their account of the journey ... Macknight kindly presented me with a copy of the rare manuscript in which it first appeared, a history of the kingdom of Gowa by Abdurrazak Daeng Patunru, *Sedjarah Goa ...* republished a few years later with the updated Indonesian spelling': at fn 6 (references omitted).

71 Lisa Palmer, *Trepang Opening Night* (February 2000) Arena Magazine http://www.arena.org.au/2000/02/trepang-opening-night> at 23 February 2010. The Opera was launched in 1997 in Indonesia and subsequently performed for four consecutive nights during the 1999 Darwin Festival.

72 *ibid.*

73 *ibid.*

74 *ibid.*

75 *ibid.*

76 *ibid.*

77 See generally, Nicholas Evans, 'Macassan Loanwords in Top End Languages' (1992) 12(1) *Australian Journal of Linguistics* 45; Nicholas Evans, 'Macassan Loans and Linguistic Stratification in Western Arnhem Land' in Patrick McConvell and Nicholas Evans (eds.), *Archaeology and Linguistics: Aboriginal Australia in Global Perspective* (1997, Oxford University Press) 237. See also Iain Davidson, 'Book Review' (2000) 35(3) *Archaeology in Oceania* 54; Ian Lilley, 'Book Review' (1998) 47 *Australian Archaeology* 75; Peter Sutton, 'Book Review' (2001) 72(1) *Oceania* 82.

78 See eg, Wayne Jowandi Barker and Barbara Glowczewski-Barker, *Spirit of Anchor* (2002, Documentary, Arnhem Land, CNRS Images/Media); *Trepang: An Indigenous Opera* (2000, video recording, Australian Broadcasting Corporation, Sydney).

79 The trade of objects 'was a mechanism through which residents of the Cobourg Peninsula could consolidate their social relationships and personal status': Scott Mitchell, 'Foreign Contact and Indigenous Exchange Networks on the Cobourg Peninsula, North-Western Arnhem Land' (1995) 2 *Australian Aboriginal Studies* 44, 47.

Stone artefacts which must have been carried into the Cobourg Peninsula have been identified in archaeological contexts. Stone artefacts from the area can be placed into two categories; those manufactured from raw materials available on the Cobourg Peninsula, and those imported from outside the region. Local materials from archaeological sites include sandstone, quartz pebbles, ferruginous quartzite and siltstone. Imported lithologies include red ochre, silcrete, gneiss, dolerite, chert, slate, vein quartz and granite. The closest outcrops of such rocks are in the Wellington ranges, some 50 km to the south-east and along the South Alligator River 75 km to the south ... Given that historic records indicate that stone artefacts were traded into the Cobourg Peninsula in return for Macassan and European objects, the archaeological trend identified on the Cobourg Peninsula was held to confirm the models of culture contact and regional exchange: at 45.

80 Peter Toner, 'Improvisation and Compositional Creativity in Yolŋu Song Texts' (Paper presented at the Symposium of the International Musicological Society, Melbourne, 12–14 July 2004) 2–4. See also Peter Toner, 'Ideology, Influence and Innovation: The Impact of Macassan Contact on Yolŋu Music' (2000) 5(1) *Perfect Beat: The Pacific Journal of Research into Contemporary Music and Popular Culture* 22, 33–4.

81 Toner, 'Improvisation and Compositional Creativity in Yolŋu Song Texts', 4.

82 *ibid* 2–3.

83 *ibid* 2–4.

84 *ibid* 2–3.

85 In 2005, I tested my assumptions about these flag emblems and their associations with clans with several Yolŋu elders. Perhaps they are the emblems of the different fleets of *perahu*, each one of which would have struck an enduring relationship with a particular Yolŋu clan by virtue of being adopted by that clan. The elders agreed that this was the case.

86 Pers. Comm. Aaron Corn, manuscript: Djaŋirrawuy Garawirrtja with Aaron Corn (Galiwin'ku, February 2005).

87 Ganter, 'Turning the Map Upside Down', 171.

88 *ibid.*

89 *ibid.*

90 *ibid.*

91 Kevin Murray, 'When it Comes to Identity, There's a Lot in a Name', *The Age News Extra* (Melbourne, Australia) 31 July 1999, 6.

92 *ibid.*

93 *ibid.*

94 See Sally May, Jennifer McKinnon and Jason Raupp, 'Boats on Bark: An Analysis of Groote Eylandt Aboriginal Bark-Paintings Featuring Macassan Praus from the 1948 Arnhem Land Expedition, Northern Territory, Australia' (2009) 38(2) *The International Journal of Nautical Archaeology* 369.

95 *Yarmirr v Northern Territory (2)* (1998) 82 FCR 533, 558 (Olney J).

96 See George Herbert Sunter, *Adventures Of A Trepang Fisher: A Record Without Romance*, (1937, Hurst & Blackett).

宣告他们仍然存在：
雍古族与望加锡历史性交流的当代延续

作者：艾伦·科恩（Aaron Corn）和阿伦·马瑞特（Allan Marett）及当吉拉武伊·嘎啦维塔（Djaŋgirrawuy Garawirrtja）

2005年8月，望加锡文化艺术团塔宾·斯瓦丽亚（Takbing Siwaliya）来访澳大利亚。其成员包括五名男音乐家和四名女舞蹈演员，将在阿纳姆丛林（Arnhem Land）东北部举办的第七届嘎玛传统文化节（Garma Festival）和达尔文艺术节（Darwin Festival）上表演。尽管各自的礼仪传统基础不同，他们的跨文化表演和澳大利亚当地雍古族人的节目一起，构成了这些活动中不可分割的部分。他们的来访，也使由来已久的阿拉弗拉海（Arafura Sea）之间的贸易来往和文化交流恢复了。雍古族和望加锡人民之间的这种交流在20世纪之前就已经持续了数个世纪。[1]

雍古族是居住于阿纳姆丛林东北部的土著"民族"，在这片地区的神圣家园中他们已居住了数千年。这里有些区域一万年前还站立海平面之上，如今已沉匿外海，而雍古族人却对它们了如指掌。在1906年南澳大利亚州州政府对海外来船课以重税之前，雍古族人一直同印度尼西亚苏拉威西岛（Sulawesi）的繁忙海港望加锡来的船员保持着广泛的联系。这些船员每年都穿过阿拉弗拉海，来到澳大利亚的北部海岸[2]。

雍古族人对这些几个世纪以来造访北部的亚洲邻居有着深入的了解。这段历史比1923年成立于阿纳姆丛林东北部米林金比（Miliŋinbi / Milingimbi）的第一个基督教传教团要早多了。他们也了解荷兰在印度尼西亚的殖民过程。17世纪中叶，望加锡的perahu，即"马来敞舱船"舰队开始每年来到澳大利亚北部海岸。其船员的目的主要是为了从澳大利亚温暖的沿海海域采摘海参，然后出售到北边遥远的中国。不过，他们也同雍古族人交换采集龟壳、珍珠、珍珠贝和木材的权利。作为交换，雍古族人获得了诸多进口商品，包括金属、斧子、糖、烟草、酒精、稻米和纺织品。有时，雍古族的男人会志愿到望加锡，在敞舱船上工作一阵，而雍古族的女人则会嫁到望加锡的家庭中，生下混血儿。

在2005年嘎玛传统文化节的第4届土著音乐和舞蹈研讨会上，来自望加锡州立大学（Universitas Negeri Makassar）的哈力林塔·拉希夫（Halilintar Lathief）发表了一篇主题演讲。他认为这些同雍古族人的历史往来十分重要，并指出在许多现存的望加锡手稿中对它们多有提及[3]。在澳大利亚内部，阿纳姆丛林东北部至今仍保留着同望加锡人接触的遗迹。望加锡人种下的罗望子树依然在澳大利亚北部海岸郁郁葱葱，在他们早先的露营地，也可以找到遗留下来的陶器和工具。

时至今日，雍古族语中仍保留了数以百计的望加锡外来语，如rrupiya"钱"、bandirra"旗子"、buthulu"子"、lipalipa"独木舟"、dhamburra"鼓"和baŋ'kulu"斧子"。在许多现存的传统雍古族 玛尼凯"歌曲"、buŋgul"舞蹈"和miny'tji"图案"的总目中，仍然记录着历史上同望加锡来访者的相互交流。[4]雍古族部族传统的玛尼凯（manikay）曲目，如达尔王古（Dhalwaŋu），就类似于阿拉伯宗教音乐中所听到的声乐旋律。特别是达尔王古部落，把先祖英雄剑客毕林尼吉（Birrinydji）的荣耀归功于同望加锡人接触的那段历史时期。[5]历史上望加锡输入阿拉姆丛林的旗子、敞舱船、锚和剑是毕林尼吉祖传力量的象征。同时，这些物品在其他将望加锡祖先人物认同为自我的雍古族部族中也很常见。雍古族流行乐团尤茶·印迪（Yothu Yindi）演唱的摇滚歌曲《望加锡船员》（'Macassan Crew'）[6]就是吸收了达尔王古和古玛提（Gumatj）部落的传统玛尼凯曲目。这首歌所歌唱的就是这些望加锡来客如何向阿拉真主祈祷，以及他们远离家乡、充满悲伤的心境。传统的雍古族葬礼仪式也体现了这种悲伤，其结尾通常是向这些来客告别的玛尼凯片断。[7]

TO PROCLAIM THEY STILL EXIST: THE CONTEMPORARY YOLŊU PERFORMANCE OF HISTORICAL MACASSAN CONTACT

By Aaron Corn and Allan Marett with Djangirrawuy Garawirrtja

In August 2005, the Macassan cultural ensemble Takbing Siwaliya, comprising five male musicians and four female dancers, visited Australia to give performances at the seventh Garma Festival in northeast Arnhem Land and the Darwin Festival. Combined intercultural performances with their Yolŋu hosts in Australia grounded in their respective ceremonial traditions, were an integral component of these events, and they reactivated a long legacy of trade and cultural exchange across the Arafura Sea that existed between the Yolŋu and Macassan peoples for several centuries prior to the 20th.

The Yolŋu are the Indigenous 'People' of northeast Arnhem Land, and have inhabited their sacred homelands within this region for countless millennia. They maintain an intimate knowledge of sites now far out to sea that are known to have been above sea level ten millennia ago, and before the State Government of South Australia began imposing costly tariffs on foreign vessels in 1906, the Yolŋu enjoyed extensive relations with seafarers from the bustling seaport, Makassar, on the Indonesian island of Sulawesi, who each year, made voyages across the Arafura Sea to Australia's northern shores.[1]

The Yolŋu had held an extensive knowledge of their Asian neighbours to the north for centuries, well before the establishment of the first Christian mission in northeast Arnhem Land at Miliŋinbi (Milingimbi) in 1923, and were aware of Dutch colonisation in Indonesia. Fleets of Makassar *perahu*, 'small craft, prahus', began visiting Australia's northern coast annually in the mid-17th century. Their crews primarily came to harvest trepang (sea cucumber) from Australia's warm coastal waters for on-sale as far north as China, yet they also traded with the Yolŋu for rights to harvest turtle shell, pearls, pearl shell and timber. In return, the Yolŋu received numerous imported goods, including metal, axes, sugar, tobacco, alcohol, rice and textiles. Sometimes, Yolŋu men volunteered to travel to Makassar for a season of work on the *perahu*, and Yolŋu woman married into Macassans' families producing children of shared descent.[2]

In his keynote address at the 2005 Garma Festival for the 4th Symposium on Indigenous Music and Dance, Halilintar Lathief from Universitas Negeri Makassar commented on the importance of these historical relations with the Yolŋu and their prominence in many surviving Macassan manuscripts.[3] Within Australia, the legacy of Macassan contact in northeast Arnhem Land also endures. The tamarind trees they seeded still grow all along Australia's northern coastline, and remnants of their pottery and tools are still found at their former campsites.

Today, the Yolŋu languages retain hundreds of Macassan loan words, such as *rrupiya* 'money', *bandirra* 'flag', *buthulu* 'bottle', *lipalipa* 'canoe', *dhamburra* 'drum' and *baŋ'kulu* 'axe', and historical interactions with Macassan visitors are recorded in many surviving traditional Yolŋu repertoires of *manikay* 'song', *buŋgul* 'dance' and *miny'tji* 'design'.[4] The traditional *manikay* repertoires of Yolŋu clans such as the Dhaḻwaŋu possess vocal melodies similar to those heard in classical Arabic religious music. The Dhaḻwaŋu clan in particular, attributes the ancestral hero Birrinydji the Swordsman to the historical period of Macassan contact.[5] The flags, *perahu*, anchors and swords that the Macassans historically imported into Arnhem Land are important icons of Birrinydji's ancestral power, and they are also common among other Yolŋu clans who recognise Macassan ancestral figures of their own. The rock song 'Macassan Crew',[6] by the

据20世纪后期古帕朋古(Gupapuyŋu)部落多子多女的酋长佳瓦·达维让古(Djäwa Dhäwirrŋu)说，曾有一位名叫努瓦(Nuwa)的望加锡船长侵入了吉利维利(Djiliwirri)的国土，许以新的生活方式。他试图说服蜜蜂先祖(Honeybee ancestor)博库达(Birrkuḍa)在那里建造房屋、建立市镇，但最后却被一大群蜜蜂包围，被迫跳入一个沸水大锅才得以逃脱。这段历史在一座传统地面雕塑的设计中也得到体现。古帕朋古部落人在葬礼后烟熏这座雕塑用于仪式净化。雕塑上有一排三个圆圈，连结着两条平行线，代表了努瓦燃起烹煮出口海参的大锅。此后，努瓦带着火柴、毯子和房屋找到犬先祖（Dog ancestor）杜兰尼杜拉(Djuranydjura)，许诺共同统治国家。但是杜兰尼杜拉拒绝了，说他已经有了拨火棍、千层板和纤维内皮桉住房，而且不管怎么说，他都拥有这个"地区。"[8]

在这个通过望加锡人，将澳大利亚同中国连接起来的繁荣跨国贸易网络中，入侵者在这些寓言中认识到了雍古族独立的重要性。不过，在嘎玛传统文化节和达尔文艺术节上带领古帕朋古舞者同塔宾·斯瓦丽亚合作的当吉拉武伊·嘎啦维塔解释说，望加锡人一般都承认长期确立的、允许他们在雍古族海滩上岸并从事贸易的协议，而不必担心有入侵的风险。他说，雍古族今天在仪式中仍然使用的彩旗制度实际上就来源于此。传统上，他们会划分海滩，允许望加锡人登上各自的海岸。不同的部落自己拥有的旗子颜色也不同：瓦拉米力(Warramiri)部落是黑色；达尔王古(Dhalwaŋu)部落是红色；古玛提(Gumatj)部落是黄色；王古瑞(Wangurri)部落是绿色；玛达帕(Maḍarrpa)部落是蓝白色；而古帕朋古(Gupapuyŋu)部落的一支博吉利(Birrkili)的则是蓝色。不论望加锡敞舱船何时在海面上出现，雍古族人都会升起相应的旗子，告知对方自己已做好贸易的准备。在达尔文艺术节上古帕朋古舞者同塔宾·斯瓦丽亚合作的两支联合曲目中，两支乐队依次演奏各自的传统曲目，再现了这种交换。

塔宾·斯瓦丽亚在2005年嘎玛传统文化节上表演传统望加锡音乐再次印证了这个说法。首席鼓手邓·迈尔 (Daeng Mile) 在土著音乐和舞蹈研讨会期间解释说，他们的演出代表了一只向外行驶中的望加锡敞舱船。音乐刚开始的*ganrang palari*"快速击鼓"摹仿船首猛烈冲开波浪，而后部*ganrang pattannang*"安静、平稳的鼓声"则表达了船员们向往家园的心境。全部演奏乐器包括一支叫做*puikpuik*的望加锡芦笛，一面叫做*kattok-kattok*的竹制狭缝鼓，以及一只小而有节的鼓，叫做 *dengkang*。四名女舞蹈员围着乐队，站立在四个方位点。她们起舞时双脚从不完全离开地面，这再一次代表了望加锡人们对苏拉威西岛深深的心灵寄托。拉希夫补充说，这四名女舞者的站位也反映了望加锡宇宙哲学中对山脉、内地、海滩和海洋的划分，以及其相应的颜色（黑、黄、红、白）与元素（土、气、风、火）。[9]

Yolŋu popular band Yothu Yindi, draws on traditional *manikay* repertoires of both the Dhaḻwaŋu and Gumatj clans. It describes how these Macassan visitors sang of Allah in prayer and how their departures for home were filled with sadness. This sadness is also reflected in traditional Yolŋu funeral ceremonies, which often end with *manikay* items that farewell such visitors.[7]

According to Djäwa Dhäwirrŋu, a prolific leader of the Gupapuyŋu clan in the latter 20th century, there was a Macassan captain called Nuwa who trespassed upon the homeland of Djiliwirri promising new ways. He tried to convince the Honeybee ancestor, Birrkuda, to build houses and create a town there, but was enveloped by a swarm of bees that would only desist after he had jumped into a cauldron of boiling water. This history is reflected in the layout of a traditional ground sculpture that the Gupapuyŋu use after funerals for ritual purification by smoking. It comprises a row of three circles connected by two parallel lines that symbolises the cauldrons that Nuwa had lit to cook trepang for export. Next, Nuwa approached the Dog ancestor, Djuranydjura, with matches, blankets and houses, and offered him joint command over the country. But Djuranydjura refused, stating that he already had firesticks, paperbark sheets and stringybark shelters, and that he owned the country' anyway.[8]

Such parables promoted the importance of Yolŋu independence from intruders amid the thriving transnational trade network that, through the Macassans, linked Australia to China. Djaṉgirrawuy Garawirrtja, who led the Gupapuyŋu Dancers in their collaborations with Takbing Siwaliya at the Garma Festival and Darwin Festival, nonetheless explains that the Macassans commonly recognised well-established protocols that permitted them to land and trade on Yolŋu beaches without the risk of trespassing. He states that this was indeed the origin of the system of coloured flags the Yolŋu still use in ceremonies to this day. Traditionally, they would mark the beaches where different clans, each with their own colour of flag, would allow Macassans to come ashore on their respective countries: black for Warramiri; red for Dhaḻwaŋu; yellow for Gumatj; green for Wangurri; blue and white for Maḏarrpa; and blue for Garawirrtja's own group, the Birrkili line within the Gupapuyŋu clan. Whenever a Macassan *perahu* appeared offshore, the Yolŋu could signal their readiness to trade by erecting the appropriate flag. The Gupapuyŋu Dancers' two combined concerts with Takbing Siwaliya for the Darwin Festival re-enacted such exchanges, with the two ensembles performing their traditional repertoires in turn.

Traditional Macassan music performed by Takbing Siwaliya at the 2005 Garma Festival complements this account. As explained by the master drummer Daeng Mile, during the Symposium on Indigenous Music and Dance, their ensemble represents an outbound Macassan *perahu* in motion. The *ganrang palari* 'fast-moving drum' out front echoes the bow as it impetuously cuts through the waves, while the *ganrang pattannang* 'calm, steady drum' at the rear maintains the crew's spiritual connection to home. The ensemble is completed by a Macassan shawm called *puikpuik*, a bamboo slit-gong called *kattok-kattok*, and a small, knobbed gong called *dengkang*. The four female dancers surrounded this ensemble, standing at the four compass points. As they danced, their feet never left the ground entirely, which again symbolises the deep spiritual connection of the Macassan people to the island of Sulawesi. Lathief added that the positioning of these four women also mirrored the divisions

Zhou Xiaoping
Red Dancing (detail)
2009
Ink, acrylic on rice paper and canvas
176 x 382cm

周小平
舞动的红裙子(细部)
2009年
水墨，丙烯，宣纸和布面绘画
176 x 382cm

1988年以来，雍古族部族屡次同他们的望加锡邻居相见。其中第一次活动由澳大利亚二百周年纪念管理局（Australian Bicentennial Authority）提供资助，庆祝1788年欧洲人在澳大利亚殖民。这多少有些讽刺意味。不过，用这笔钱，埃尔科岛（Elcho Island）上的雍古族部落噶力温库（Galiwin'ku）庆祝了一个历史更为悠久的事件。在这个事件中，一只传统木制敞舱船一路漂洋过海从望加锡来到那里，并登上了海滩。在噶力温库的海滩上，这只小艇受到了当地整个部落的欢迎。部落人欢欣地举行了一场传统仪式，标志望加锡人等待已久的回归。10

在古帕朋古舞者和塔宾·斯瓦丽亚于2005年达尔文艺术节上结束了最后一场演出的当日，他们接受了采访。在采访中，当吉拉武伊·嘎啦维塔细说了双方合作的这两周以来他们之间相互的亲密关系。嘎啦维塔提到了这里是博吉利·古帕朋古的家乡龙古恰(Luŋutja)，就是在这里，古时的望加锡访客将上岸同蓝色旗子之下的雍古族人进行贸易。他也提到了他们穿越而过的芒古入(Muŋurru)的周围海域：

是的，我们紧挨的邻居、朋友、亲戚的来访真是了不起。这是个划时代的事件。它把我带回了那个年代，那时我的博吉利·古帕朋古祖先和我的望加锡兄弟姐妹们在一个叫做龙古恰的地方相会。当我们昨晚重演这个仪式，我感觉自己回到了那个年代。不知何故，我感觉自己的血液中，先辈的血液中，都深深地流淌着这个仪式。我们彼此无间。我们的联系紧密不分。我们的需求相差无几。我们的内心几乎一致。

我们在机场道别时，我感觉自己似乎回到了当时祖先们在龙古恰海滩相见的情景。我人在达尔文机场，却仿佛身处龙古恰，感觉自己的灵魂回到了龙古恰海滩。当他们彼此告别，我想象他们迎着 maḏirriny "西南风"，会一路顺风。因为，基本上我所演奏的是芒古入，是我的海水，而我的风是 maḏirriny 风，将他们的敞舱船带回望加锡的家。这正是在风向转北之前；正是在被称作 Luŋurrma 的北风刮起之前。

在嘎玛传统文化节和达尔文艺术节那些我们相处的日子里，他们似乎生活在那些古老的岁月中，而我们也在追溯初期的航海时代。是风告诉了我，他们何时动身出发最为适宜。并且我觉得我所唱的每支歌曲，我的祖先们所唱的每支歌曲，基本上都为这交流史的最后章节划上了圆满的句号。我们今天所感受到的一切，我们的泪水与坚强、悲伤和告别，和我们祖先的所感所想是完全一致的。因此，即使我身处达尔文国际机场，我的心依然飞回到了龙古恰海滩，向赶在风向改变之前搭上顺风船的人们告别。

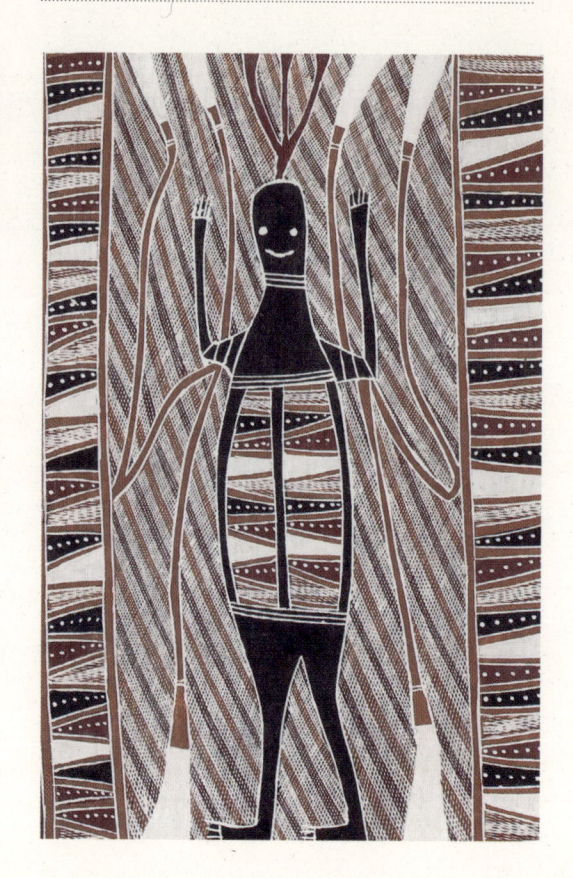

among the mountains, the hinterland, the beach and the sea within Macassan cosmology, along with their corresponding colours (black, yellow, red and white) and elements (earth, air, wind and fire).⁹

Since 1988, Yolŋu communities have been united with their Macassan neighbours on several occasions. The first of these was, somewhat ironically, funded by the Australian Bicentennial Authority, which had been created to celebrate the establishment of permanent European settlement in Australia in 1788. However, the event mounted with these funds by the Yolŋu community of Galiwin'ku on Elcho Island celebrated an even longer history, with a traditional wooden perahu sailing all the way from Makassar and landing there on the beach. It was met on the beach at Galiwin'ku by the entire community, who jubilantly performed traditional ceremony to mark the Macassans' long-awaited return.¹⁰

In the following interview conducted on the day after the Gupapuyŋu Dancers' final concert with Takbing Siwaliya at the 2005 Darwin Festival, Djaŋgirrawuy Garawirrtja describes the special bond shared by these two ensembles over the fortnight of their collaboration. Garawirrtja mentions here the Birrkili Gupapuyŋu homeland of Luŋgutja where Macassan visitors of old would come ashore to trade with Yolŋu under the blue flag, and the surrounding waters of Muŋurru through which they sailed:

Yeah, that visit from our next-door neighbours, our friends, our relations, was really something. It was a landmark. It took me back to the time when my Birrkili Gupapuyŋu ancestors met my Macassan cousins at the place called Luŋgutja. When we performed that ceremony last night, I found myself back in those times. Somehow, I felt it deeply through my blood, and through the blood of my forefathers. We were very close. Our contact was very close. Our needs were very close. Our inner being was almost the same.

When we said our last farewells at the airport, I found myself back in the time when our ancestors met on that beach at Luŋgutja. Even though it was at Darwin Airport, I felt it was at Luŋgutja and that, spiritually, I was there at Luŋgutja beach. Watching them departing, I thought of them getting that tailwind from the madirriny 'south-westerly wind'. Because basically, what I was performing was my Muŋurru, my saltwater, and my wind is the madirriny wind that sends their perahu on its way back to their home in Makassar. It came just before the wind swung around to the north; before the northerly wind, which is called Luŋgurrma, blew.

During those days that we were together at the Garma Festival and during the Darwin Festival, they were living in those ancient days, and we were also accessing that earlier maritime age. It was the wind that told me when it was the right time for them to leave, and I felt that every song that I had been singing, and my forefathers sang, basically wrapped up this latest chapter in our history of contact. The feelings, and the tears and strengths, and sorrows and farewells, were just the same as in those early times. So even though I was at the international airport in Darwin, in spirit I was at Luŋgutja beach saying farewell as they caught the last tailwind before the wind changed.

John Bulunbulun
Trepang-Bunapi (detail)
2009
Ochre pigments with PVC fixative on stringybark (Eucalyptus tetradonta)
115.5 x 79.2cm

约翰·布龙·布龙
海参-Bunapi (细部)
2009年
树皮，PVC定色剂，天然色素
(四齿桉)
115.5 x 79.2cm

那些日子离我们并不遥远。那些时代离我们并不遥远。不过,时代变了,也许在未来他们会从另一个方向乘风而来,与我们相见。我们将看见他们从另一个风向,即 *bärra'* "西边"而来。*Bärra'* 刮起的日子就是他们上岸的时候。这是到来,不过,说到离开,他们会赶上 *ma<u>d</u>irriny* 风,也就是南风,将他们推向其他的海上航线。

嘎啦维塔继续描述这种深厚的远祖共鸣如何充满整个合作的过程。古帕朋古舞者试着用 *bi<u>l</u>ma* "双棒"和 *yi<u>d</u>aki* "迪吉里杜管(didjeridu)"合奏,而舞蹈员则随塔宾·斯瓦丽亚的音乐起舞。

我们花了十天时间才弄明白他们的节奏类型和我们的之间有怎样的联系。十天之后,我开始掌握了他们鼓的节奏。这些节奏同我们的玛尼凯类型相似,也和我们所演奏的节奏类型模进类似。那些跳舞的雍古族女士也开始掌握到诀窍,掌握到下一个出现在模进中的节奏会是怎样的。这模进和我们的模式是一致的。比如我们有个节拍的次第叫做 *dhudi-nhirrpan* "基础",就是单拍缓击,我们还有个连续拍子组成的序列叫做 *yindi* "响亮"。当我完成一段节奏的模进,他们知道应当在哪里加入。当他们听到迪吉里杜管类型,就知道加入。

昨天,他们开始加入越来越多兴奋的节奏。我们也加入了。他们加入了额外的力度,我们也照做,这样音乐就在最后达到了高潮。当他们敲击最后部分的鼓点节奏,提示我和团员站起,我注意到听众中有一对夫妇觉得很奇怪,为什么没有接到任何提示我们就知道站起。他们肯定不会相信,我们是在倾听对方的鼓点。所以我们站起时我看到有几位听众挠头表示不解。怎么会呢?这怎么做到的呢?这是不可能的。但是,这就是心有灵犀。这就是因为我们一开始就回到了过去的那段时日。我们触及了"基础",触及了所追求力度的极限,并且加入了额外的力量。

我们感到悲伤,因为我们即将离去。我们看到邓·迈尔,他是老板和领队之一。击鼓的时候他感动地哭了。从根本上说,他触及了那片大地的底部、那个"基础",触及到了大地的力度,因此流下了泪。为同一个原因,我们全都泪流满面。我们的心灵相通。我们以某种方式彼此相连。这真是不可思议,不是吗?所以,当我们为国家和 *dalkarra* "远祖力量"做最后的祈祷,实际上就是指这一切都将属于我们。当我们以这种方式祈求大地,它意味着我们将再次相聚,就像半个月前那样。通过 *dalkarra* 我们不仅宣告了自己的存在,也宣告了他们的存在。

We live by those days. We live by those times. But times change and we might catch them again if, in the future, they arrive on another wind. We'll see them coming from another wind direction, called *bärra'* 'west'. *Bärra'* is when they come ashore. That's for the arrival, but for the departure, they would catch the *na<u>d</u>irriny* wind, which is the southerly wind that pushed them toward the other sea route.

Garawirrtja goes on to describe how this deep ancestral affinity informed the collaborative process as the Gupapuyŋu Dancers found ways to make their ensemble of voices, *bi<u>l</u>ma* 'paired sticks', *yi<u>d</u>aki* 'didjeridu'[11] and dancers work alongside the music of Takbing Siwaliya.

It took us about ten days to work out how their rhythmic patterns related to ours. After ten days, I started to pick up their drum patterns. They were like patterns in our *manikay*, like the sequences of rhythmic patterns that we do. The Yolŋu ladies who danced were also picking up what they were doing, and what rhythm would come next in the sequence, which accorded with our principles. Like we have a sequence of beating with slow single taps called *dhu<u>d</u>i-nhirrpan* 'foundation', and then a sequence of continuous taps called *yindi* 'big'. When I was finishing my sequence of rhythms, they knew where they should come in. When they heard the didjeridu pattern, they knew to come in.

Then yesterday, they began to add more and more excitement, which we shared. They put in extra energy and we put in extra energy, and so we managed to achieve a climax at the end. I noticed that when they did their last drum patterns to alert me to stand up with my people, a couple in the audience were wondering why we were standing up without any notification. They couldn't believe that we were reading their drum patterns. So we stood up and I saw a few of the audience scratching their heads. How come? How could that be? That's impossible. But that was the spirit. That was because we were all back in that time at the beginning. We touched that foundation. We'd touched the bottom of that depth we'd sought, and we'd all put some extra energy into it.

We felt sad because they were going to leave. We saw one of the bosses, one of the head leaders, Daeng Mile. He was so moved that he was crying while he was playing his drum. Basically, he touched the bottom of that ground, the foundation, the depth of that ground, and from his tears, we got the same tears too. We had the same. We connected with that thing. Somehow we connected. It was amazing, you know? So when we did that final invocation of country and its *<u>d</u>alkarra* 'ancestral power', we actually meant that all this will be ours. When we invoke the land in this way, it means that we have to meet again another day as we did two weeks ago. By proclaiming through the *<u>d</u>alkarra* that we still exist, we were also proclaiming that they still exist.

Dr Aaron Corn (PhD Melb)
ARC Future Fellow and Associate
Professor of Ethnomusicology
ANU School of Music, The Australian
National University

Emeritus Professor Allan Marett
University of Sydney
Director of the National Recording Project
for Indigenous Performance in Australia.

Dja<u>n</u>girrawuy Garawirrtja
Birrkili Yolŋu Elder

END NOTES

1. Charles Campbell Macknight, *The Voyage to Marege': Macassan Trepangers in Northern Australia* (1976, Melbourne: Melbourne University Press); Yumbulul Yunupiŋu, and Djiniyini Dhamarra<u>n</u>dji, 'My Island Home: A Marine Protection Strategy for Manbuyŋa ga Rulyapa (Arafura Sea)', in Galarrwuy Yunupiŋu (ed.), *Our Land is Our Life: Land rights—past, present and future* (1997, Brisbane: University of Queensland Press) 181–187; Buku-Larrŋgay Mulka Centre, *Saltwater: Yirrkala Bark Paintings of Sea Country* (1999, Sydney: Isaacs).

2. Macknight, *The Voyage to Marege'*; Michael Cooke (ed.), *Aboriginal Languages in Contemporary Contexts: Yolŋu-Matha at Galiwin'ku* (1996, Batchelor: Batchelor College).

3. D Carment (ed.), *2005 Garma Festival Key Forum Report* (1006, Darwin: CDU Press) 32–5.

4. Ronald M and Catherine H Berndt, *Arnhem Land: Its History and Its People* (1954, Melbourne: Cheshire); Peter M Worsley, 'Early Asian Contacts with Australia' (1955), 7 *Past and Present* 3–4; Donald Thomson, 'Early Makassar Visitors to Arnhem Land and Their Influence on Its People' (1957) 23 *Walkabout* 29–31; WL Warner, *A Black Civilisation: A Social Study of an Australian Tribe*, rev. ed. (1969, New York: Harper) 455–8; Ian S McIntosh, 'The Dog and the Myth Maker: Macassans and Aborigines in Northeast Arnhem Land' (1994) 9 *Australian Folklore*, 77–81; Ian S McIntosh, 'Islam and Australia's Aborigines? A Perspective from Northeast Arnhem Land' (1996) 20 *Journal of Religious History* 53–77; Michael Cooke (ed.), *Aboriginal Languages in Contemporary Contexts: Yolŋu-Matha at Galiwin'ku* (1996, Batchelor: Batchelor College) 1–20; Peter G Toner, 'Ideology, Influence and Innovation: The Impact of Macassan Contact on Yolŋu music' (2000) 5 *Perfect Beat* 22–41; Aaron Corn with Neparrŋa Gumbula, 'Djiliwirri Ganha Dhärranhana, Wäŋa Limurruŋgu: The Creative Foundations of a Yolŋu Popular Song' (2003) 7 *Australian Music Research* 64–5.

5. Peter G Toner, 'When the Echoes Are Gone: A Yolŋu Musical Anthropology', (2001, PhD. Australian National University) 2–4.

6. Yothu Yindi, 'Macassan Crew', *Garma*, Mushroom, MUSH332822 (2000), track 1.

7. Aaron Corn, *Reflections and Voices: Exploring the Music of Yothu Yindi with Mandawuy Yunupiŋu* (2009, Sydney: Sydney University Press) 47–52.

8. Keen, Ian 'One Ceremony, One Song: An Economy of Religious Knowledge among the Yolŋu of Northeast Arnhem Land' (1978, PhD. Australian National University) 61–5; Aaron Corn, with Neparrŋa Gumbula, 'Ancestral Precedent as Creative Inspiration: The Influence of Soft Sands on Popular Song Composition in Arnhem Land' in Graeme Ward & Adrian Muckle (eds), *The Power of Knowledge, the Resonance of Tradition: Electronic Publication of Papers from the AIATSIS Conference, September 2001* (2005, Canberra: AIATSIS) 55–62.

9. R Anderson Sutton, 'Tradition Serving Modernity? The Musical Lives of a Makassarese drummer' (2006) 37 *Asian Music* 1–23; Carment, *2005 Garma Festival Key Forum Report* 32–5.

10. Ian S McIntosh, 'Islam and Australia's Aborigines? A Perspective from Northeast Arnhem Land' (1996) 20 *Journal of Religious History* 74; Corn with Gumbula, 'Ancestral Precedent as Creative Inspiration' 47–8; Stephenson, Peta, 'Andrish Saint-Clare and the *Trepang* Project: The "Creative Intermediary" in an Indigenous–Asian Theatrical Production', (2008) 32 *Journal of Australian Studies* 163–78.

11. The term didjeridu is the English name used to denote the musical instrument *yidaki*, a long hollowed out tree trunk used in a woodwind style by continuous breathing and blowing.

81

82

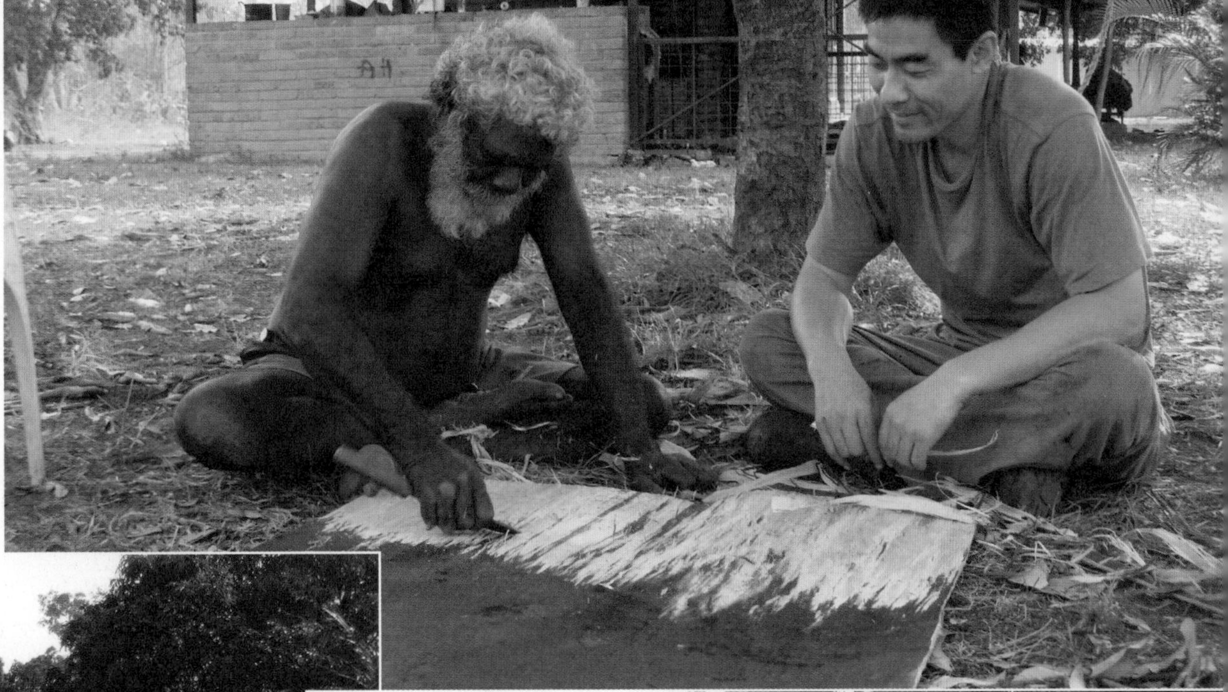

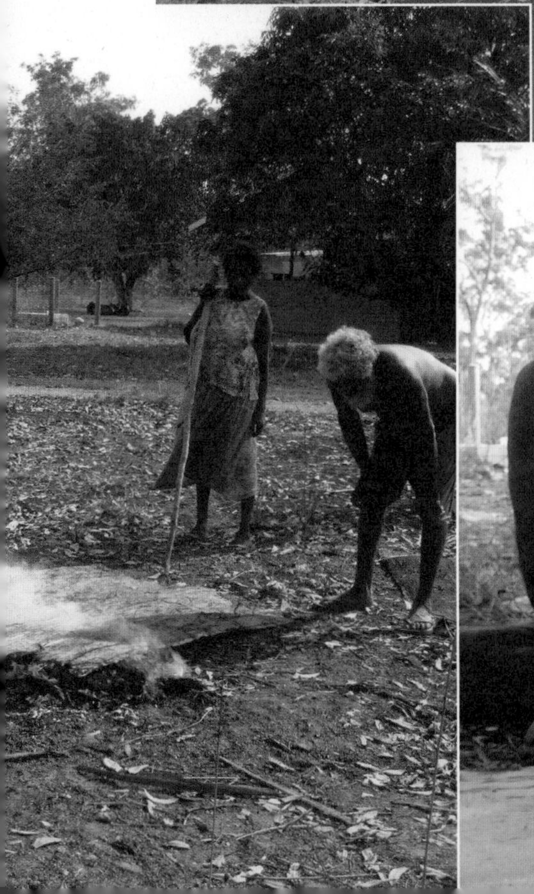

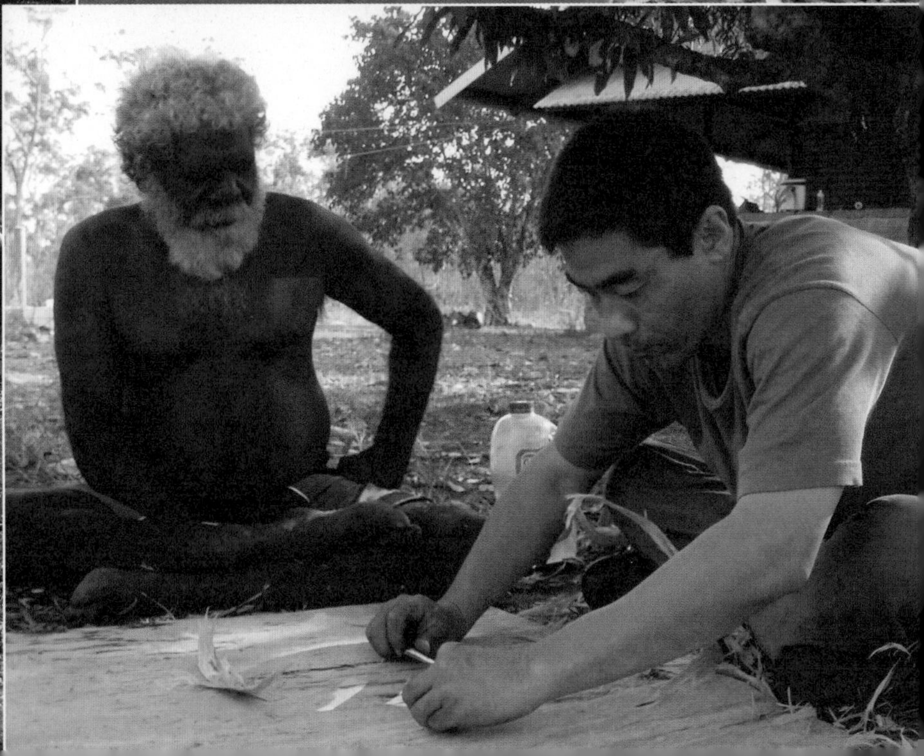

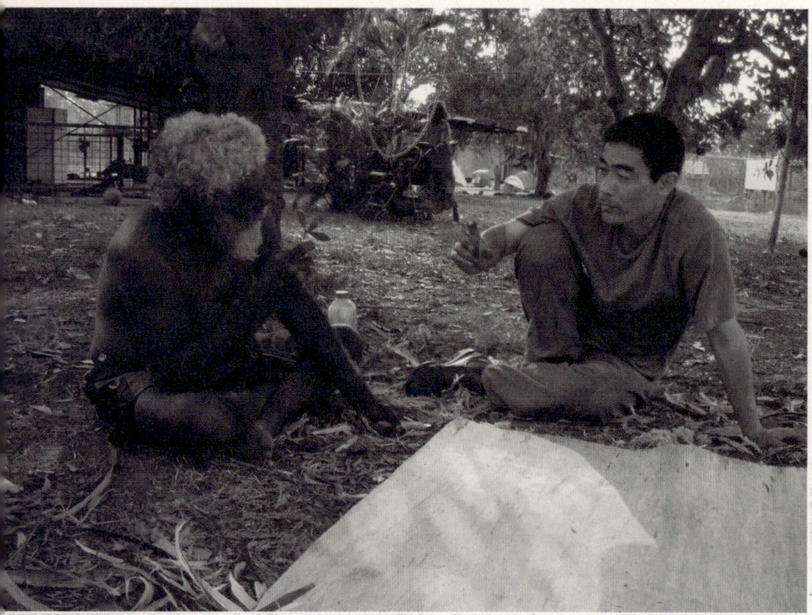
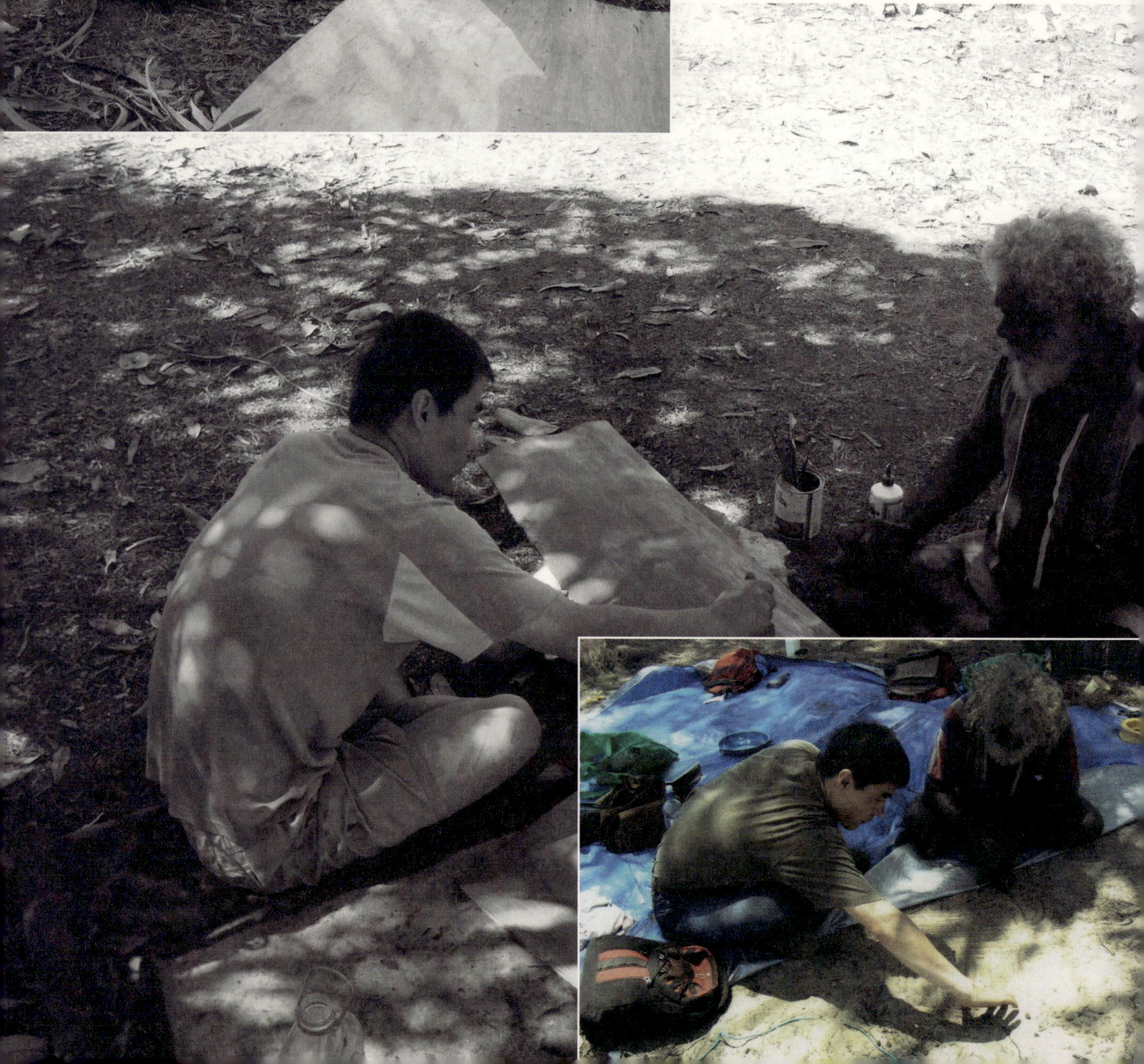

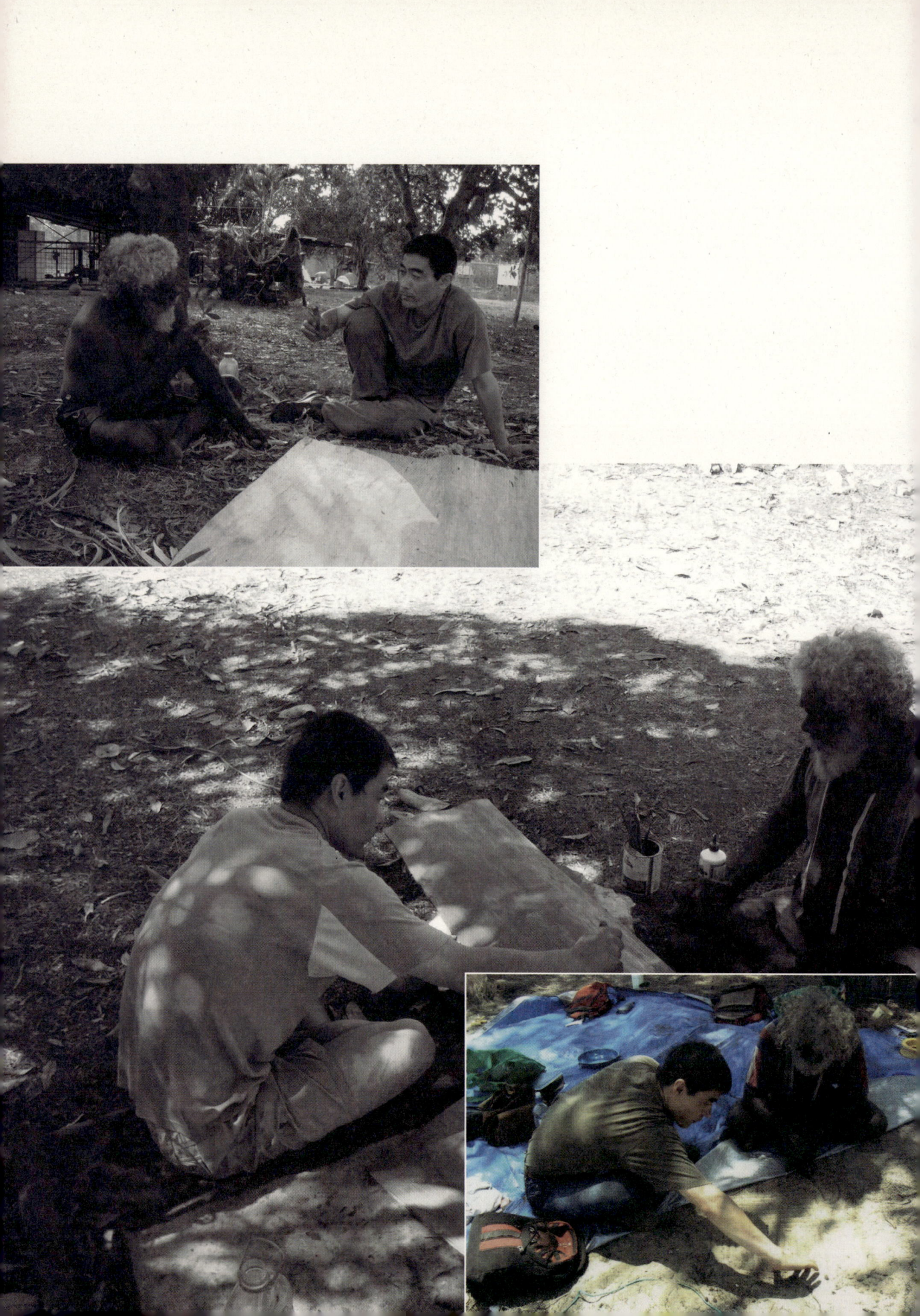

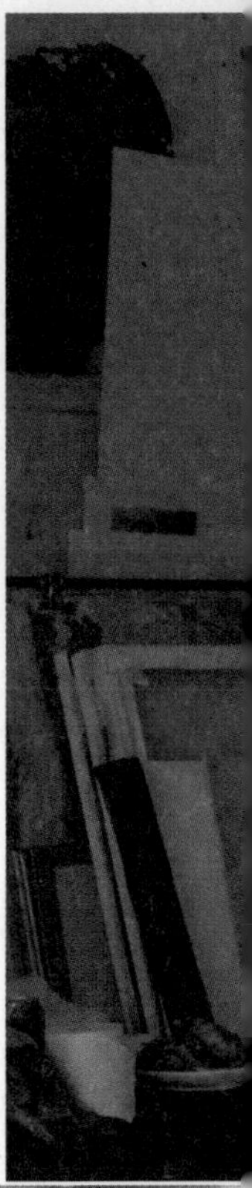

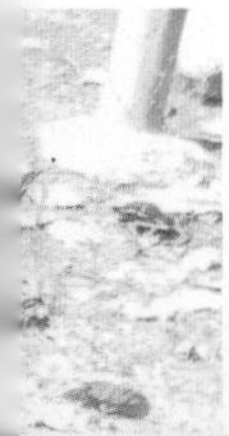

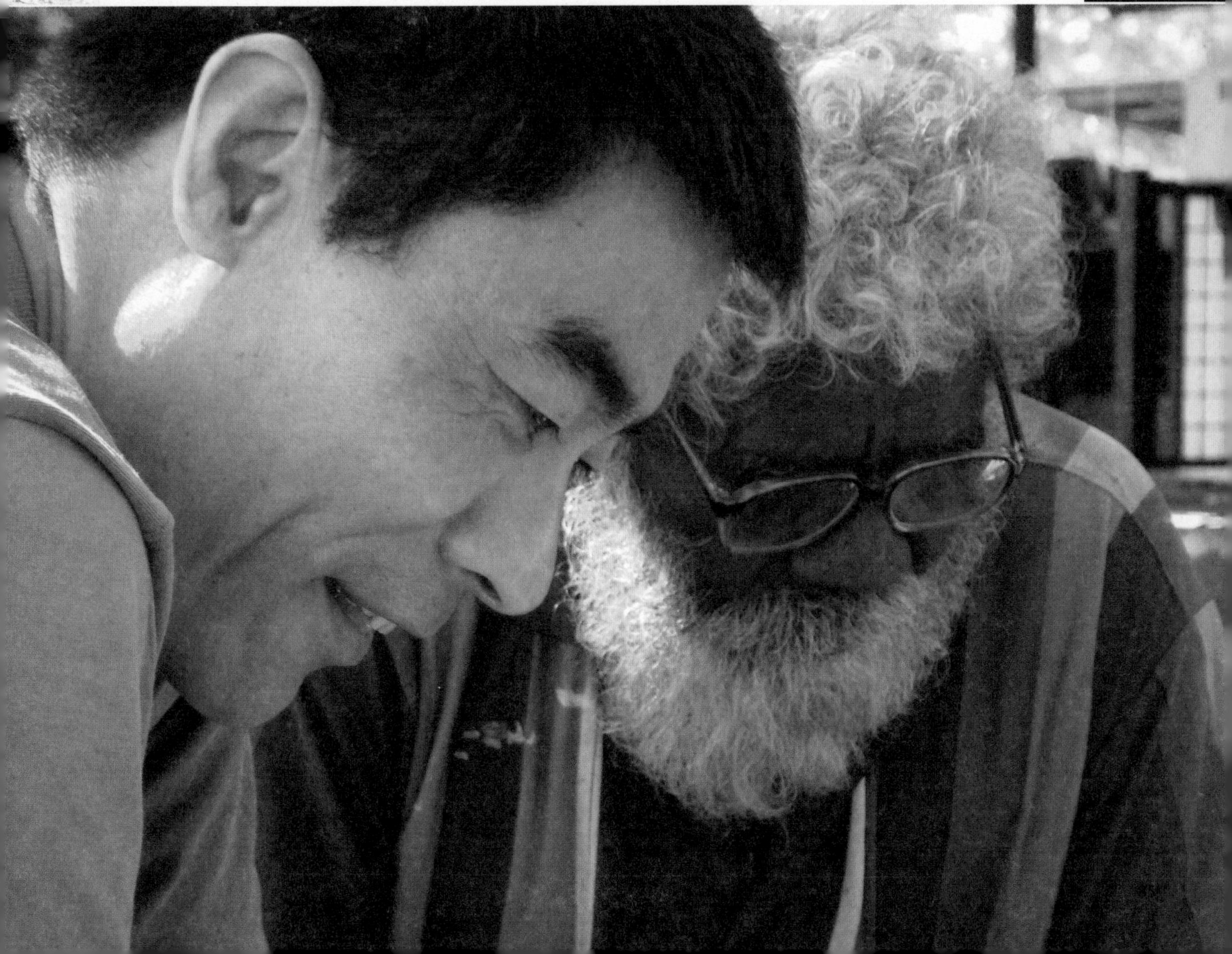

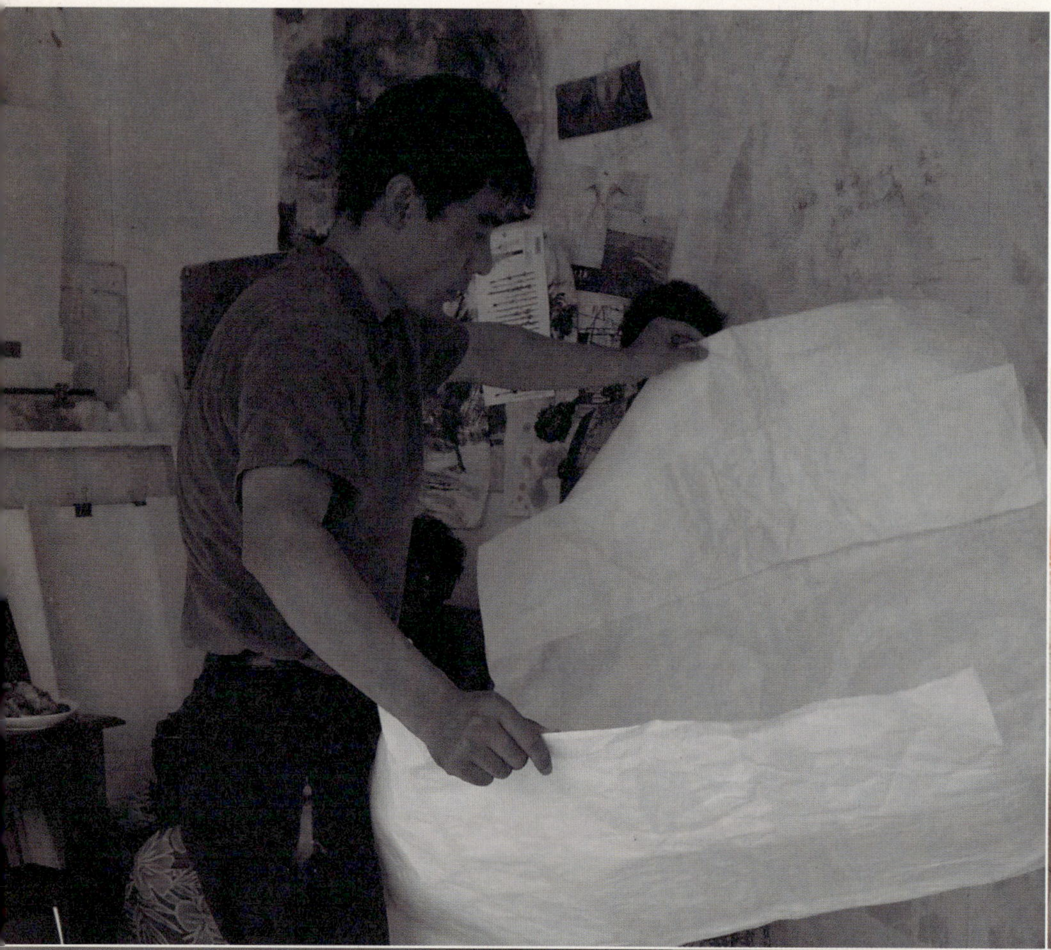

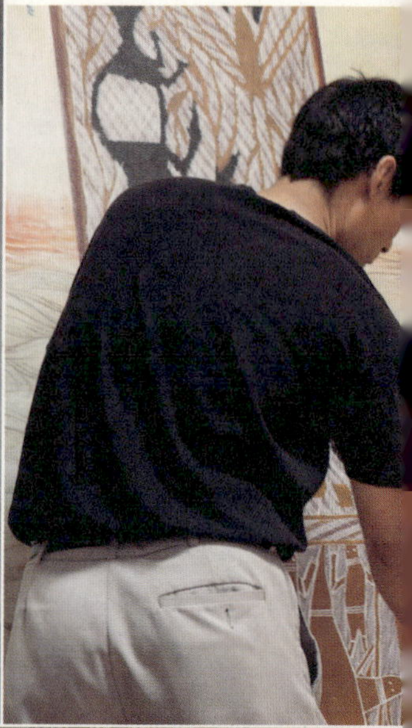

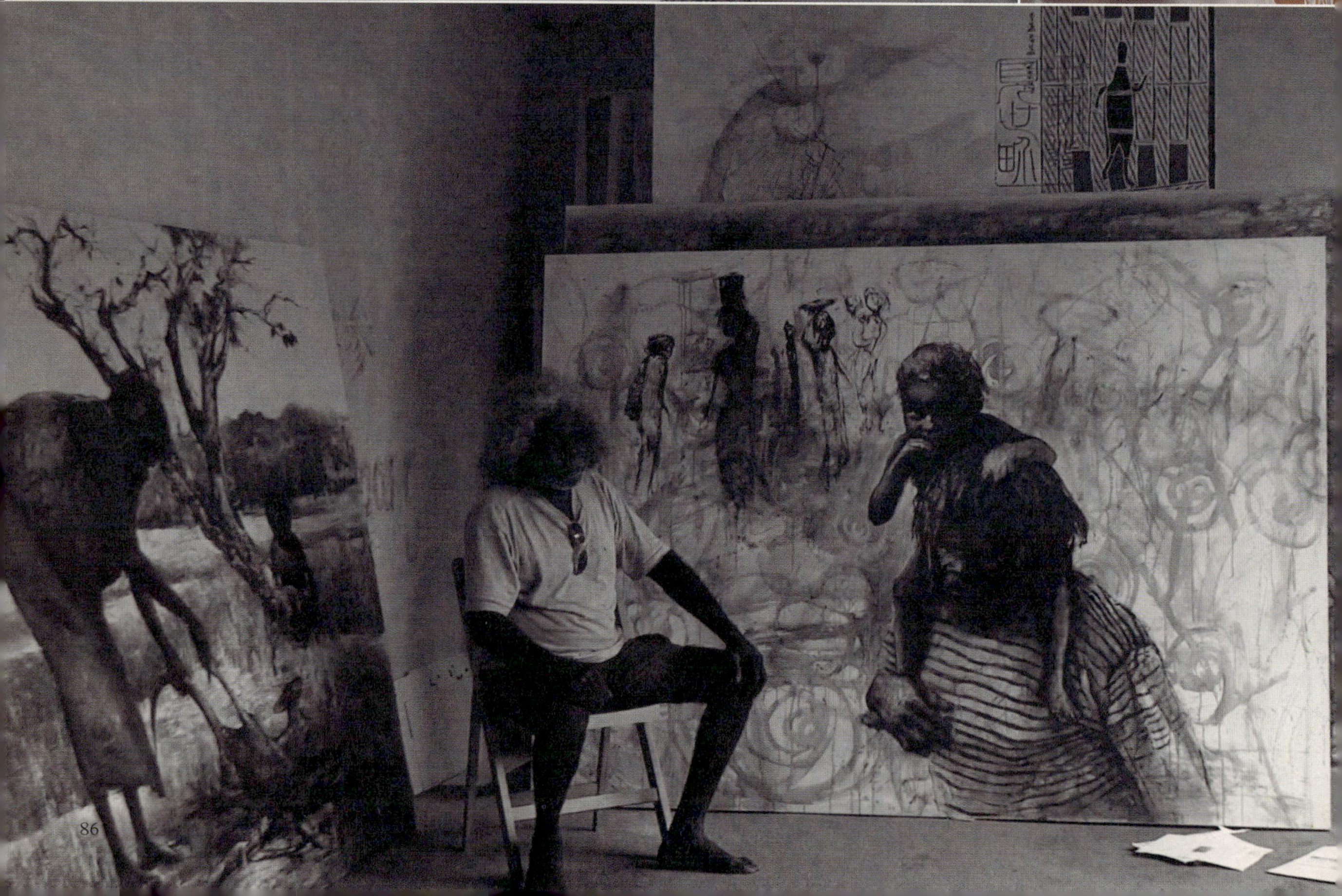

87

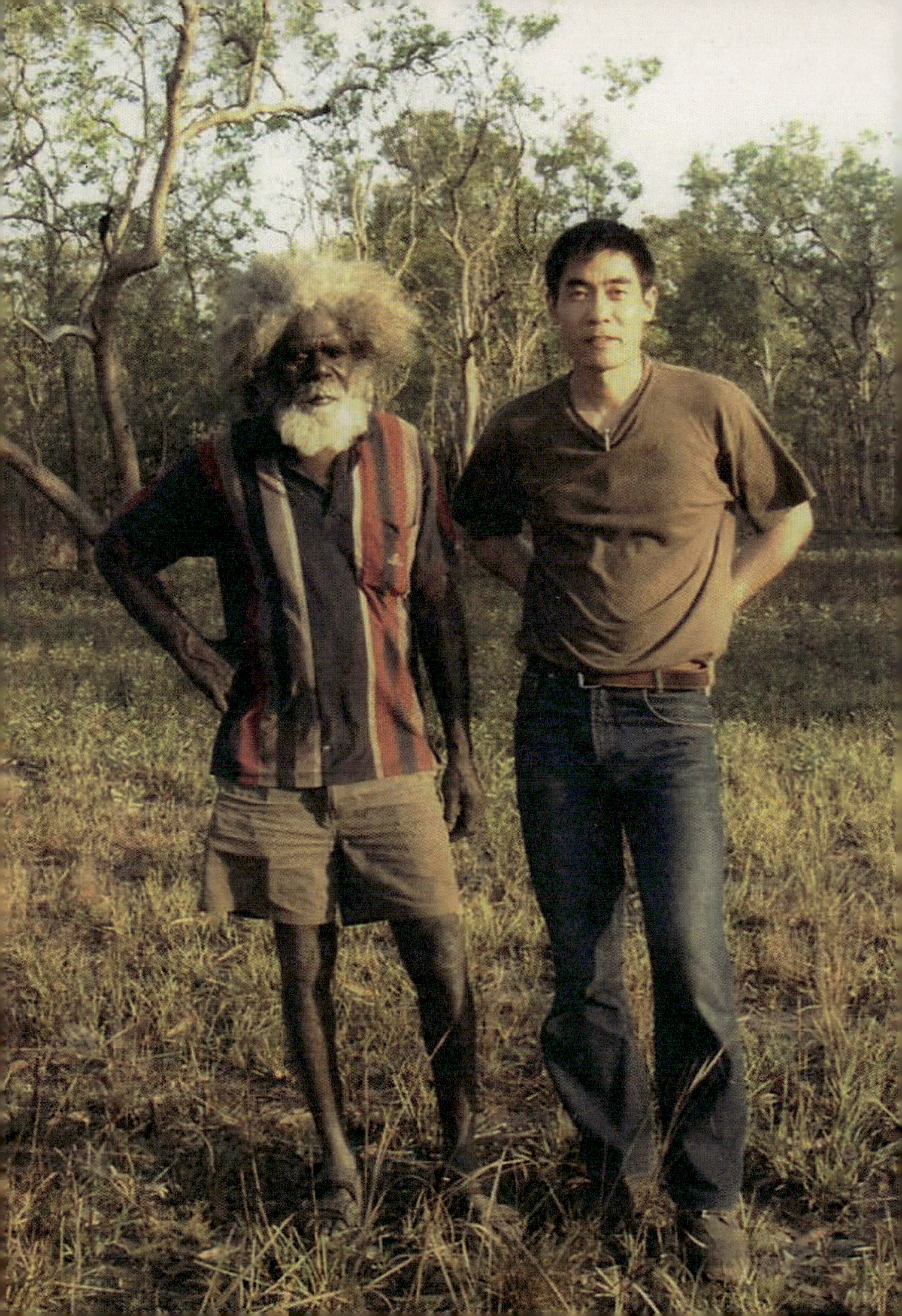

Zhou Xiaoping
Untitled History
2009
Bark and rice paper
170 x 190cm

周小平
没有标题的历史
2009
树皮和宣纸
170 x 190cm

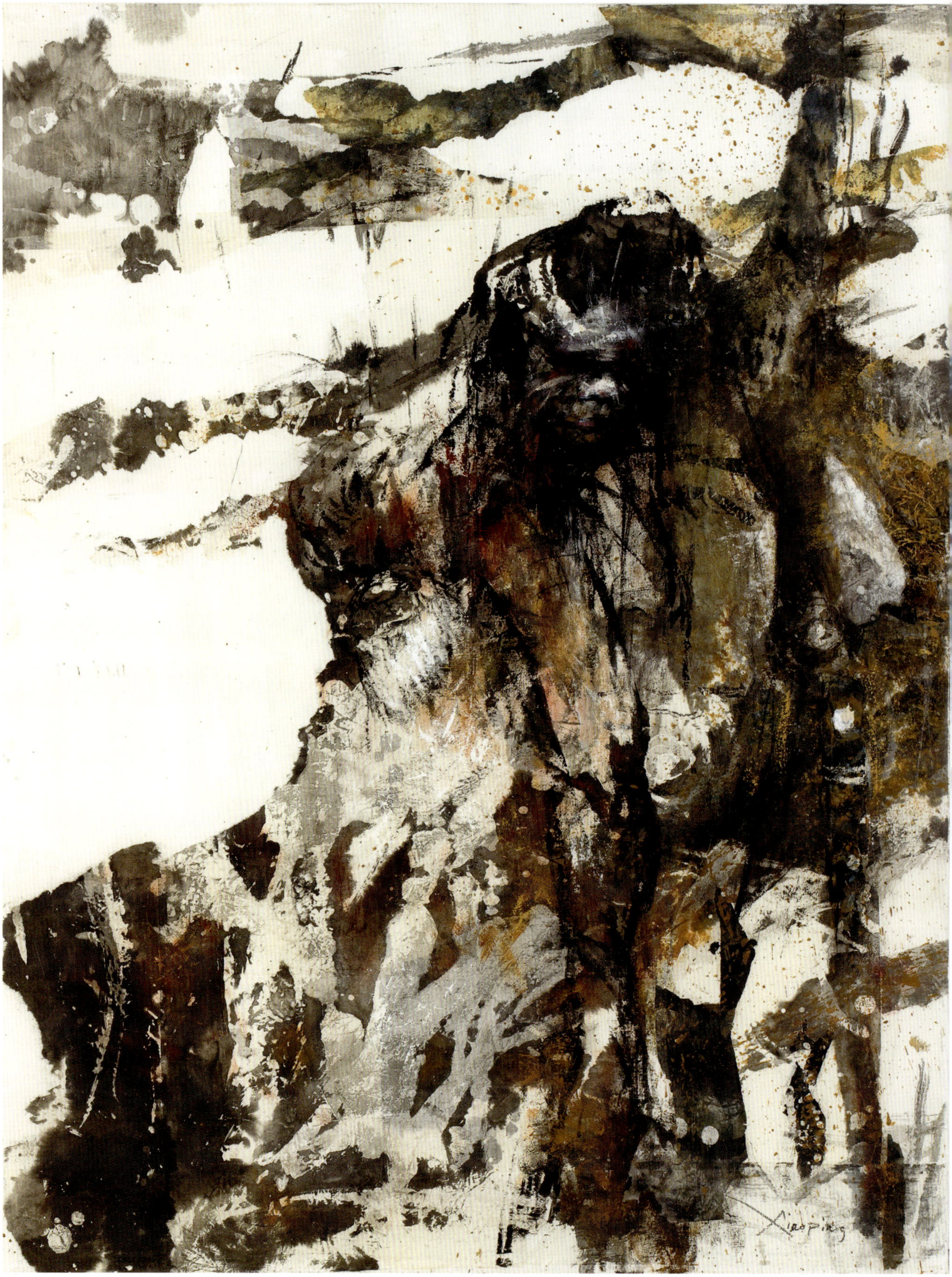

Zhou Xiaoping
Rock Men
2009
Ink, acrylic on rice paper
175.5 x 131.6cm

周小平
合一
2009年
水墨,丙烯,宣纸和布面
绘画
175.5 x 131.6cm

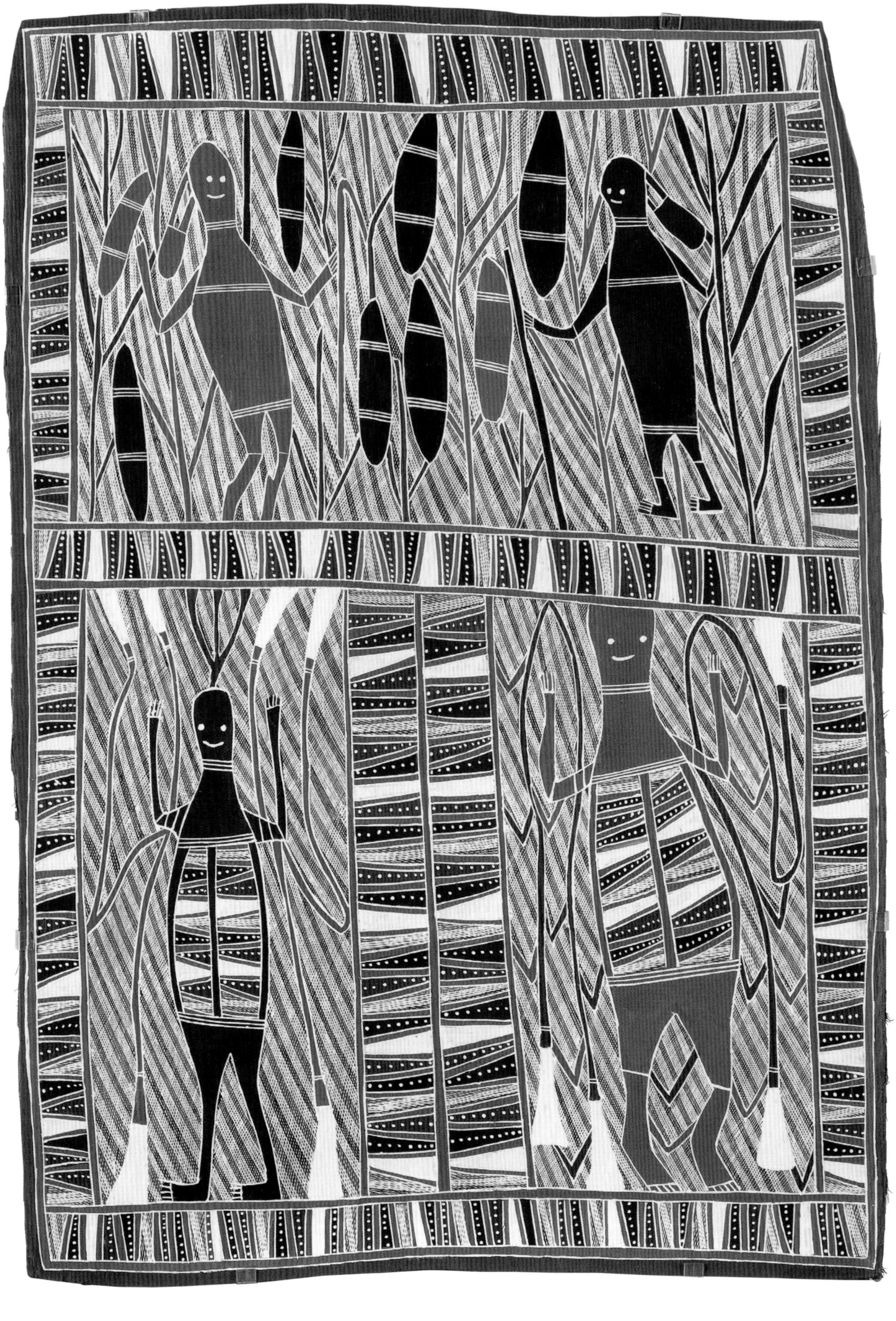

John Bulunbulun
Moiety: Yirritja
Clan: Gurrambakurramba
Trepang-Bunapi
2009
Ochre pigments with PVC fixative on stringybark (Eucalyptus tetradonta)
15.5 x 79.2cm

约翰·布龙·布龙
部落分支：Yirritja
部落：Gurrambakurramba
海参-Bunapi
2009年
树皮，PVC定色剂，天然色素
(四齿桉)
15.5 x 79.2cm

这是一幅描绘海参商人与lunggurruma设计的图画。Lunggurruma是Ganalpingu族及其相关部落对澳大利亚北部干旱季节中晚期下午海洋西北风的叫法。这种设计画在参加 *djapi* "成年礼"、murrakundja、Ganalpingu族公共外交仪式及各类丧葬仪式等场合的Ganalpingu男人身上。

Lunggurruma之所以如此重要，是因为它是Ganalpingu各种宗教理念核心精髓的象征符号。其中一点涉及的是主风向改变的重要性，标志着一年四季季节的轮换。对采猎民族而言，全国各地的食物供给及流动与季节变换紧密相关，人类对世界的认知也包含了对季节变换标志的熟稔。季节变换推动了生命的延续及自然界的丰饶，这些都是土著仪式与视觉艺术的重要主题。而lunggurruma的来临，更是长时间干热气候过后季风雨到来的前兆。

Lunggurruma 也是 Ganalpingu 族 Murrakundja公共外交仪式的核心元素。这项仪式歌颂的是区域部落与来自苏拉威西的望加锡海参渔民之间漫长的友好关系。几百年来，望加锡船都会乘着西北季风运道而来，整个湿季期间都呆在这里，并在雨季结束时风向转为东南风时返回苏拉威西。Murrakundja仪式上举行一系列与lunggurruma相关的宗教主题，其中有个场景是一个身上装着lunggurruma设计的舞者爬上仪式举办场中央的大树。据说这棵树是lunggurruma树，而爬树的舞者则象征着在形成期间一直围着树盘旋的风。

布龙·布龙说，构成lunggurruma设计的四种颜色 —— galatjal "黑"、gamanungku "白"、miku "红"及 butjalak "黄"，象征着四个Yirritj分支：Bangardi、Bulany、Gojok和Ngarritj。每个Yirritja人都隶属于其中的一个分支。

©Maningrida
艺术与文化版权所有。

This is a painting of the Trepang people and the lunggurruma design. Lunggurruma is what people from the Ganalpingu group and their related clan groups call the wind that blows from the north-west over the sea in the late afternoon during the mid to late dry season in the northern part of Australia. This design is painted on the bodies of Ganalpingu men during ceremonies such as djapi 'young man's initiation', murrakundja, the Ganalpingu group's public diplomacy ceremony, and for various mortuary rituals.

The significance of lunggurruma derives from its status as a symbolic emblem central to a number of aspects of Ganalpingu religious thought. One of these relates to the importance of the changes in the prevailing winds that mark the transitions of seasons throughout the seasonal cycle. For a hunter-gather people, food availability and movements around different parts of country are closely tied with the changes in seasons, and people's knowledge of their world involves an intimate understanding of the indicators of seasonal change. Seasonal change is what drives the continuation of life and the fertility of the natural world, and these are important themes in Aboriginal ceremony and visual art. The arrival of lunggurruma is especially marked as it heralds the onset of the monsoonal rains after a long period of dry hot weather.

Lunggurruma is also central to the Ganalpingu's public diplomacy ceremony called Murrankundja. This ceremony celebrates the long association between people of their regional group with the Macassan trepang fishermen from Sulawesi. For several hundred years Macassan boats would arrive on the north-west monsoon winds, stay throughout the wet season and return to Sulawesi when the prevailing winds swung around to the south-east at the end of the rainy season. The Murrakundja ceremony enacts a number of ritual themes associated with lunggurruma, including one stage of the ceremony when a dancer wearing the lunggurruma body design climbs a tree placed in the centre of the ceremony ground. This tree is said to be the lunggurruma tree, and the dancer climbing it is like the wind that swept across up and around the tree during its creation.

Bulunbulun says that the four colours that comprise the lunggurruma design - galatjal 'black', gamanungku 'white', miku 'red' and butjalak 'yellow' - stand for the four Yirritja subsections: Bangardi, Bulany, Gojok and Ngarritj. Every Yirritja person falls into one or other of these subsections.

© Maningrida
Arts & Culture

Zhou Xiaoping
Red Dancing
2009
Ink, acrylic on rice paper
and canvas
176 x 382cm

周小平
舞动的红裙子
2009年
水墨，丙烯，宣纸和布面
绘画
176 x 382cm

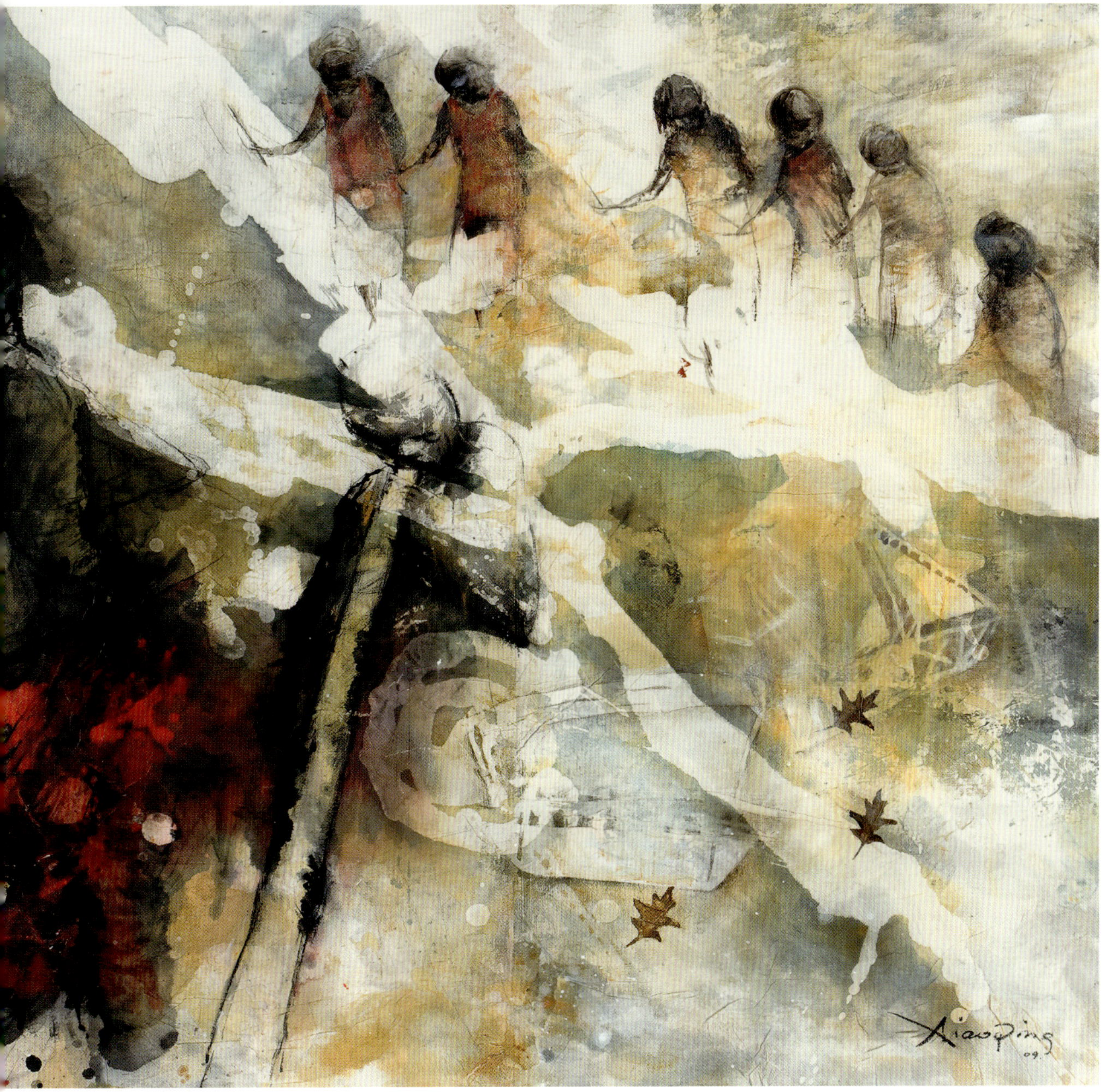

John Bulunbulun
Trading with Macassans
2008
Ochre on canvas
169 x 327cm

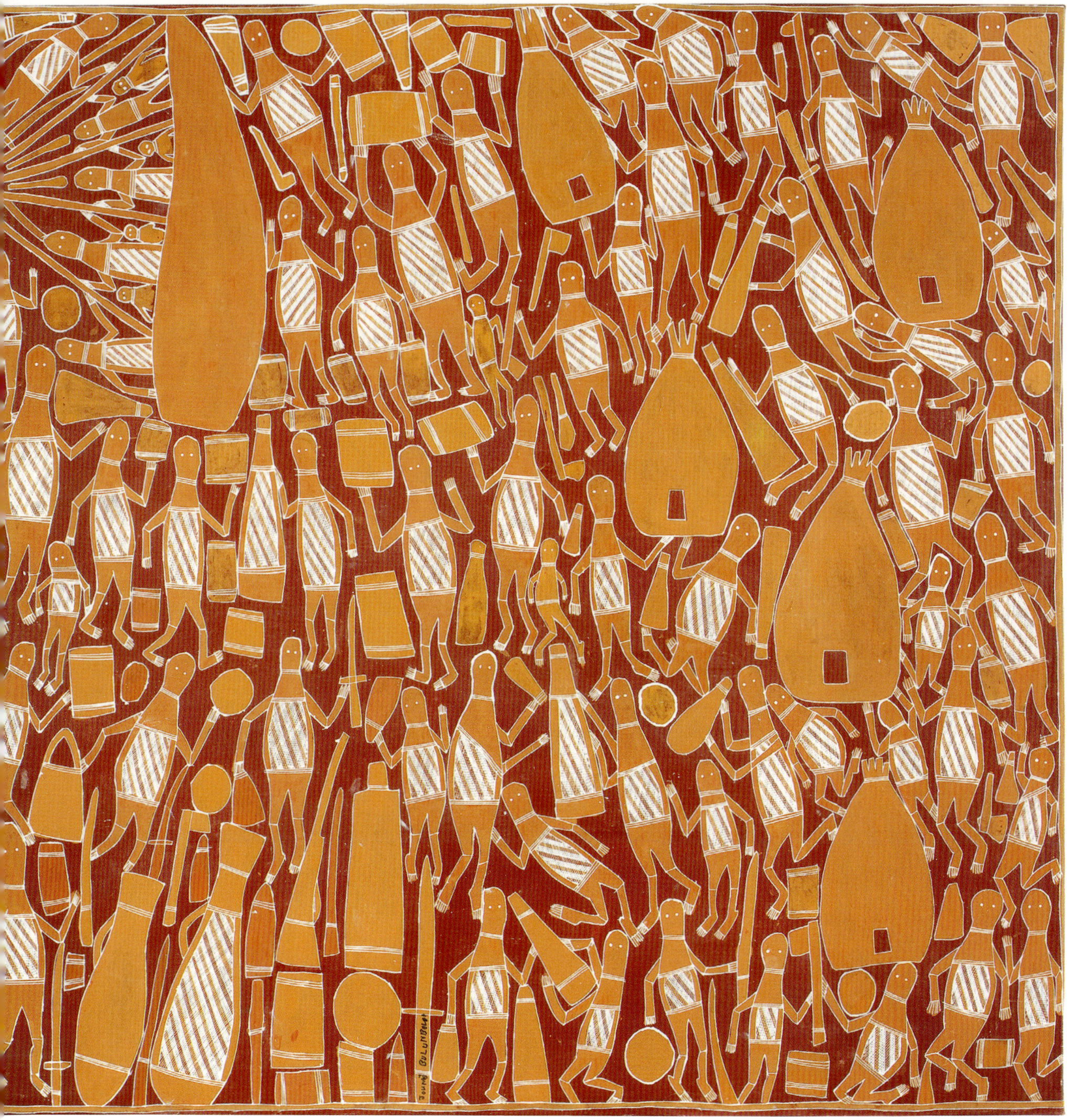

Zhou Xiaoping
Sacred black (2)
2002
Ink on rice paper and canvas
173 x 289.5cm

周小平
神圣的黑色 *(2)*
2002年
水墨，宣纸和布面绘画
173 x 289.5cm

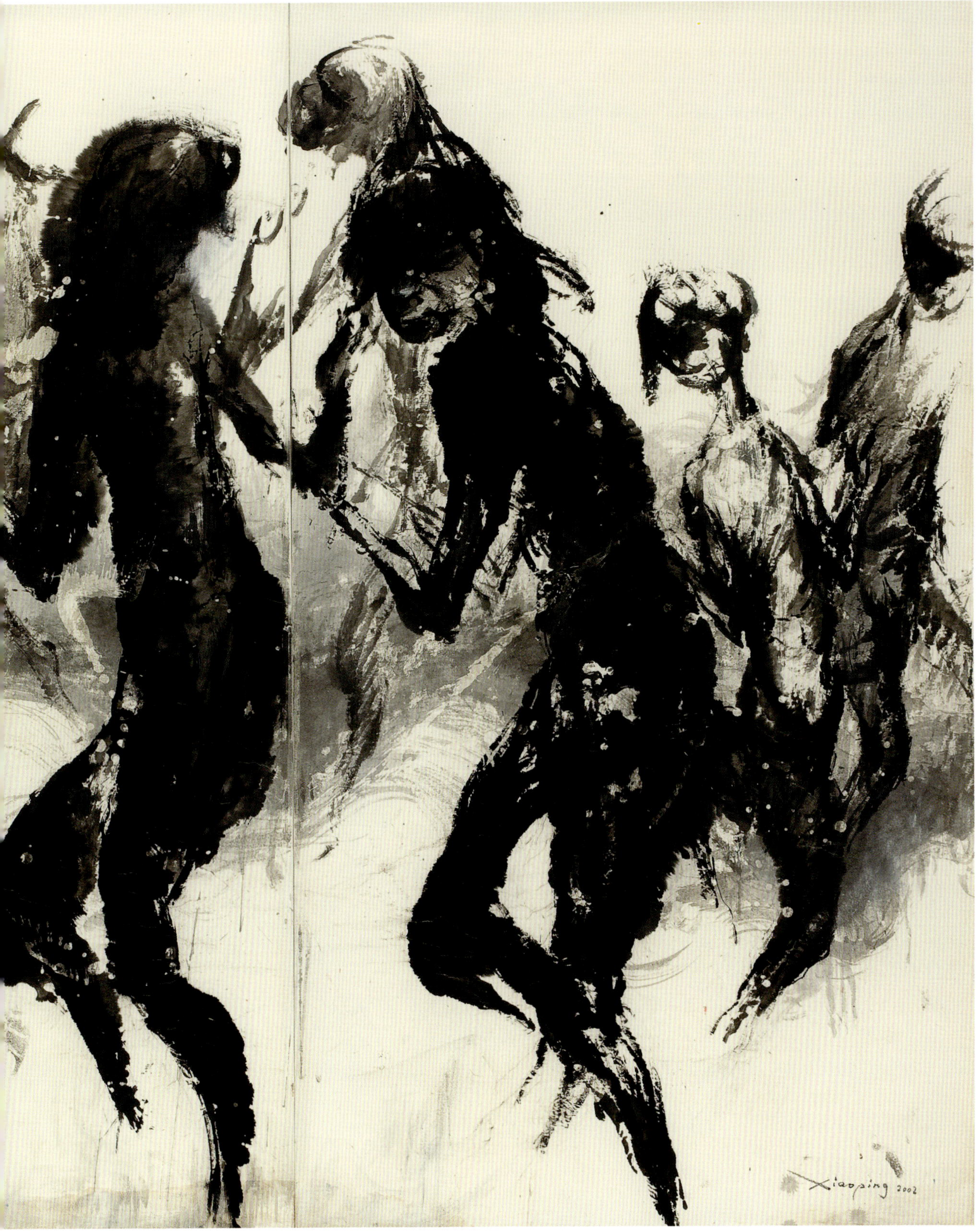
Xiaoping 2002

Zhou Xiaoping
String pulled across time ----
---a journey continues
2009
Acrylic on canvas
169.3 x 169.3cm x 2 panels

周小平
跨越时空之线
2009年
丙烯，布面绘画
169.3 x 169.3cm x 2版

海参交易线路图

Zhou Xiaoping
Trading
2010
Installation scales, trepangs
250 x 1500cm

周小平
交易
2010年
材料：秤，海参
250 x 1500cm

105

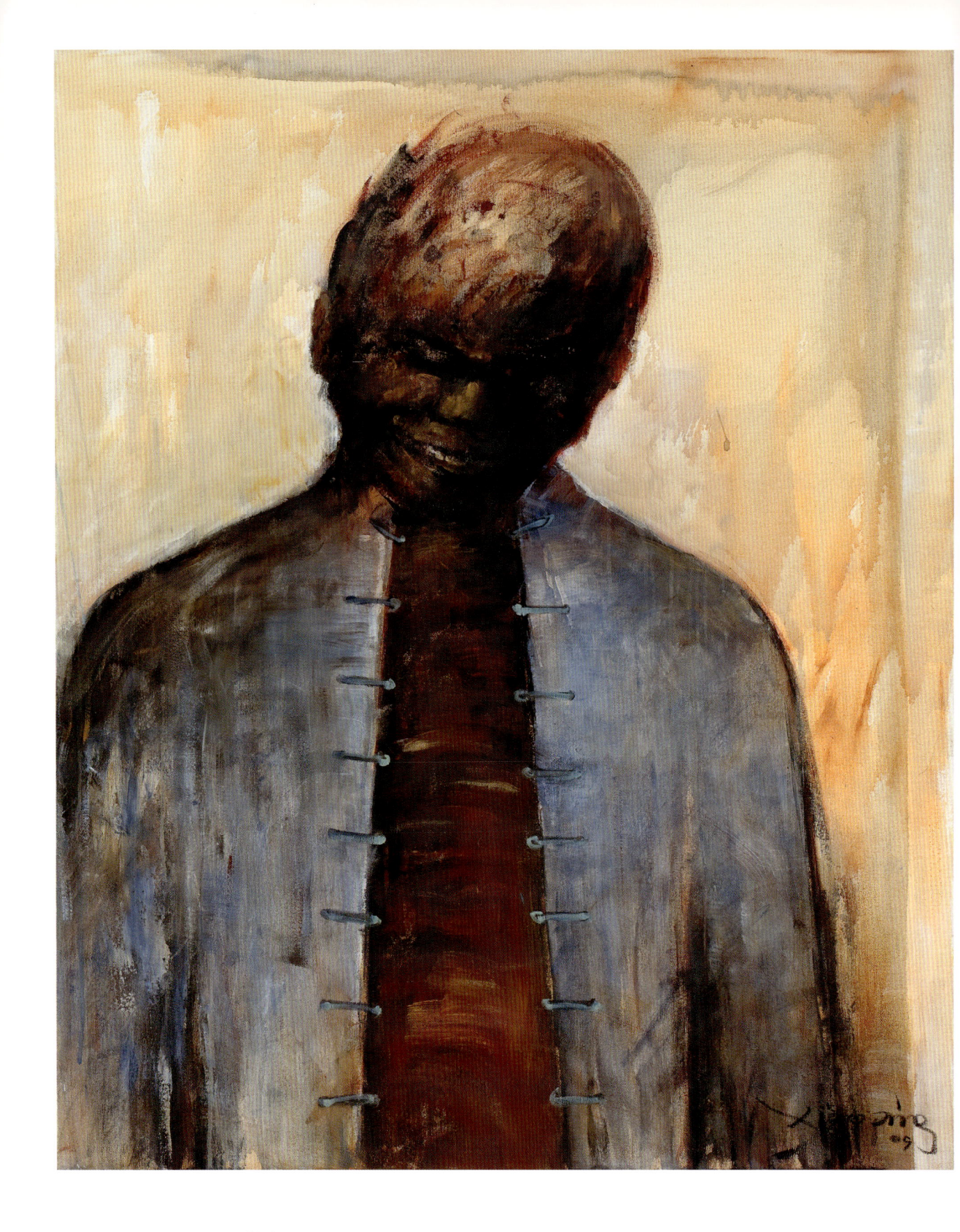

Zhou Xiaoping
Complacent (一)
2009
Acrylic on canvas
118 x 95cm

周小平
得意 (之一)
2009年
丙烯，布面绘画
118 x 95cm

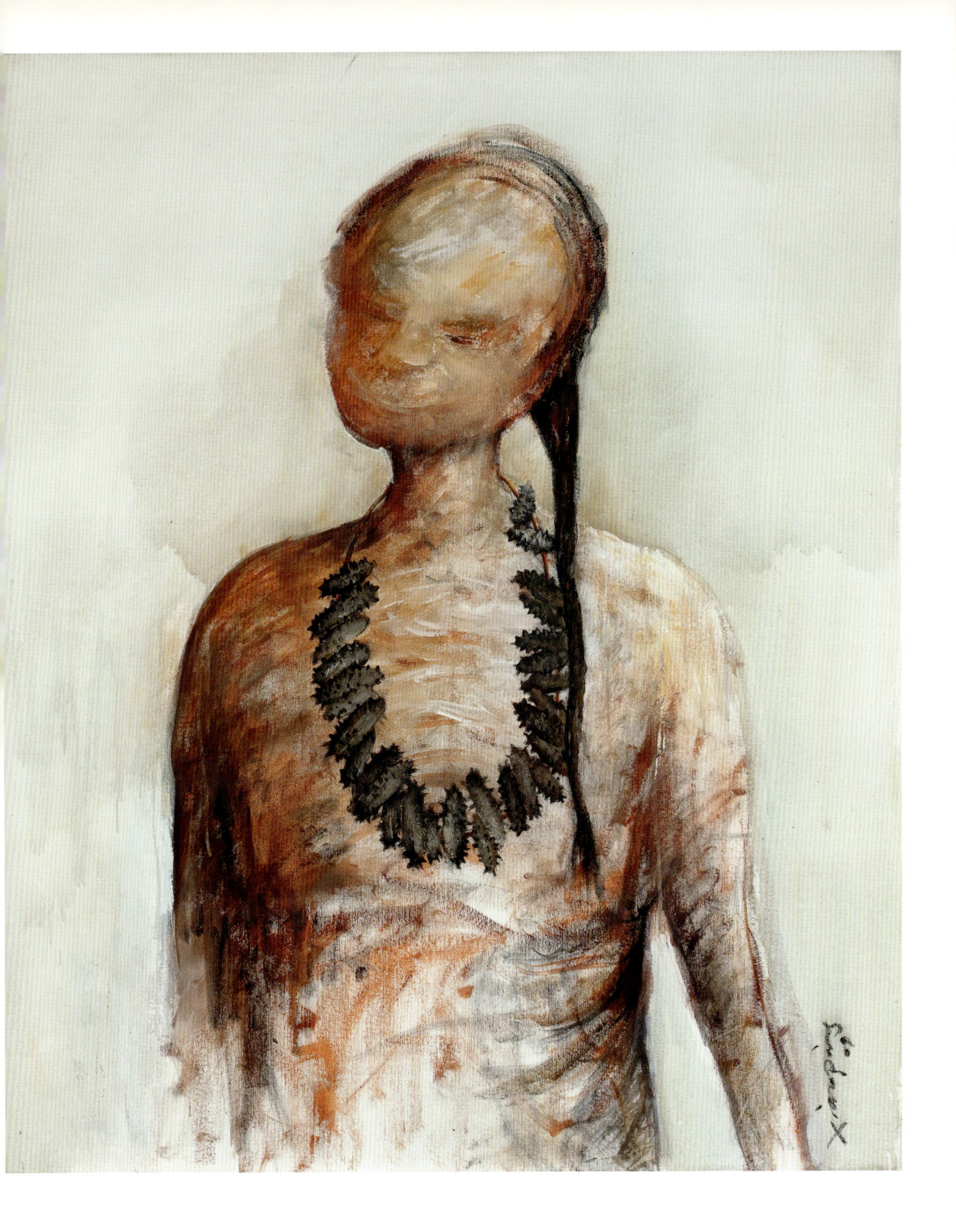

Zhou Xiaoping
Complacent (二)
2009
Acrylic on canvas
118 x 95cm

周小平
得意（之二）
2009年
丙烯，布面绘画
118 x 95cm

聖賢夢難醒
民日出

Zhou Xiaoping
Thinker
2010
Oil on canvas
200 x 165cm

周小平
思想者
2010年
布面油画
200 x 165cm

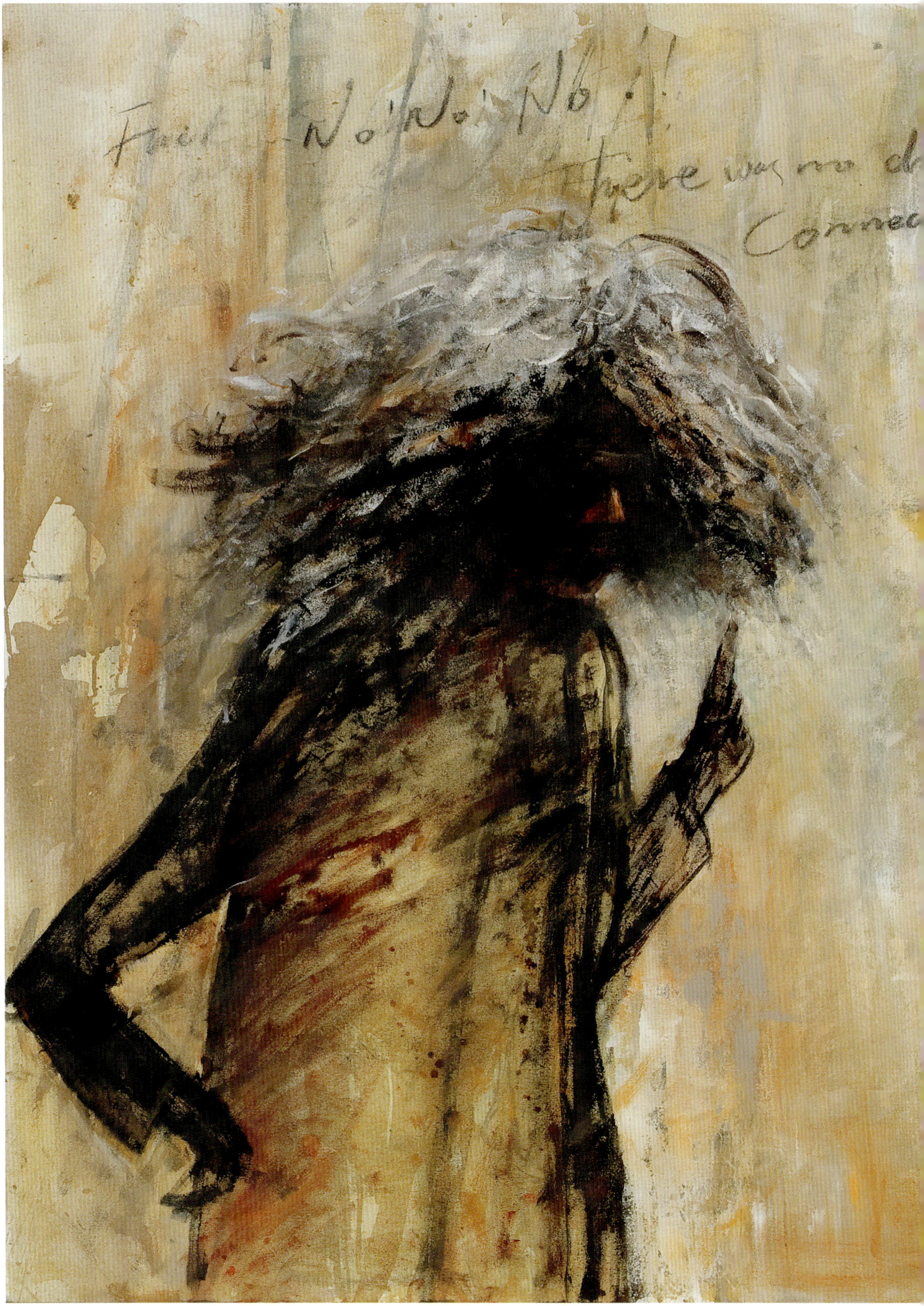

Zhou Xiaoping
Why not?
2009
Acrylic on canvas
123.8 x 164.5cm

周小平
为什么不呢?
2009年
丙烯,布面绘画
123.8 x 164.5cm

John Bulunbulun
& Zhou Xiaoping
From art to life
2009
Ink, acrylic and ochre
on rice paper and canvas
170 x 285cm

约翰·布龙·布龙和周小平
回归生命
2009年
水墨，丙烯，天然色素，宣
纸和布面绘画
170 x 285cm

113

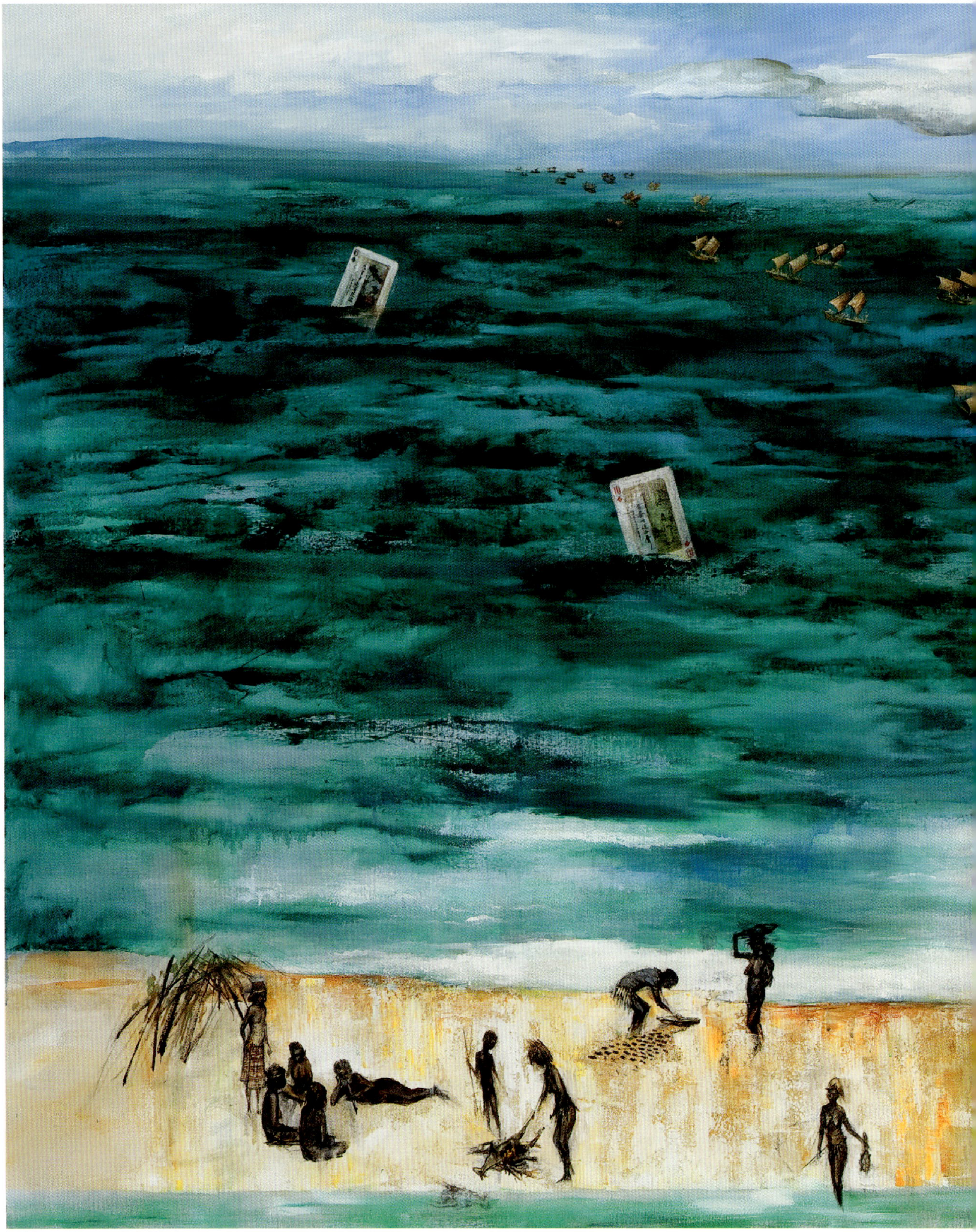

Zhou Xiaoping
Journey starts from here
2009
Acrylic on canvas
160 x 270cm

周小平
一切从这里开始
2009年
丙烯，布面绘画
160 x 270cm

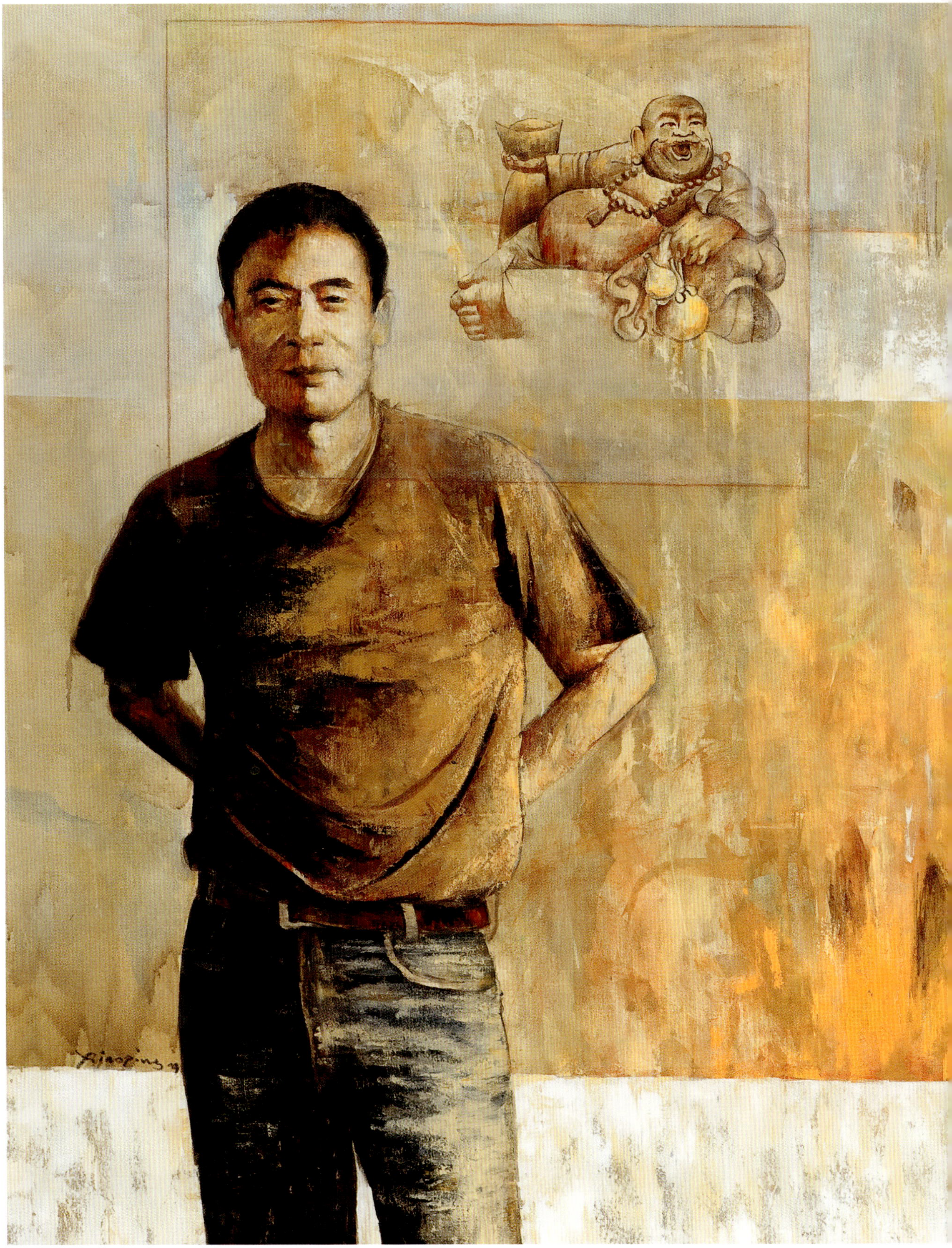

Zhou Xiaoping
How Johnny sees me
2009
Acrylic on canvas
169 x 265cm

周小平
约翰眼中的我
2009年
丙烯，布面绘画
169 x 265cm

第116-117页的说明

2008年John Bulunbulun与他的家人来墨尔本，临走前我带著他們去商场购物，一圈走下来布龙·布龙始终没有看中他钟意的东西。

最后他却对我说："Gojok,我想要一個菩萨。"

这让我想到几天前我们曾在路边的橱窗里看到过一尊弥勒佛。

布龙·布龙的要求让我吃惊，在我的认知里菩萨是"闻声救苦"，"有求必应"的神明。

但在布龙·布龙的心中"菩萨"又意喻着什么？

布龙·布龍對我說："我希望他可以为我带来幸运。"经过他的一番解释，我终于明白，他希望回到土著部落群后，在未来的牌局中能赢上几把。玩牌是他們日常生活中主要的社交娱乐。

通过这件事他给我的触动是，許多时候大家都在关注描述象布龙·布龙这样的土著人，但是人们却很少去思考，他们又是如何在看周围的人和事呢？

对于一个淳朴世界的原住民而言，用摄影机，捕捉他们的狂想及快乐，他们最希望在這个世界中"狩猎"到什么？对于久居于城市社会中的人们而言，一旦涉身于神秘的和未被开发的神圣领地，"大家"又希望"狩猎"到什么？从我这个东方面孔的人身上他又看到了什么呢？

从易位、转换、交易和交流中，两者有了接触与交往，有了合作与冲突，有了商業和文化，更有了艺术和历史。

——周小平

Previous

In 2008 John Bulunbulun and his family came to Melbourne. Before they left I took them shopping; after walking around Bulunbulun still hadn't found anything he liked.

However at the end he told me: "Gojok, I want a Buddha."

This reminded me of the Laughing Buddha statue we saw a few days ago in a shop window by the road.

Bulunbulun's request surprised me, according to my understanding the Laughing Buddha is a god who was 'a saviour to those in need' and who 'never refused a prayer'.

But what did 'Buddha' mean to Bulunbulun?

Bulunbulun told me: "I hope he can bring me luck." After he had explained, I finally understood. He hopes that after he returns to his Aboriginal tribe, he might win a few hands in future card games. Card games are the main social entertainment for them.

Through this episode what touched me was, for a lot of the time everyone has been interested in describing Aborigines like Bulunbulun, but people have rarely considered, how do they see the people and things around them?

For an indigenous person who lives in an unsophisticated world, if they used a camera to capture their wildest dreams and happiness, what would they wish to 'hunt' for the most in this world? For people who have long lived in an urban society, once they are submerged in a mysterious and undiscovered holy ground, what does 'everyone' wish to 'hunt' for? What does he see in a person with an Asian face?

Through changing places, transformation, exchanges and communication, the two peoples have made contact and communicated, they have cooperated and faced each other, they have traded and shared cultures, but even more they have created art and history.

Zhou Xiaoping.

John Bulunbulun
& Zhou Xiaoping
portray of John Bulunbulun
2007
Acrylic and ochre
on canvas
200 x 147cm

约翰·布龙·布龙和周小平
约翰·布龙·布龙的肖像
2007年
丙烯，天然色素，布面绘画
200 x 147cm

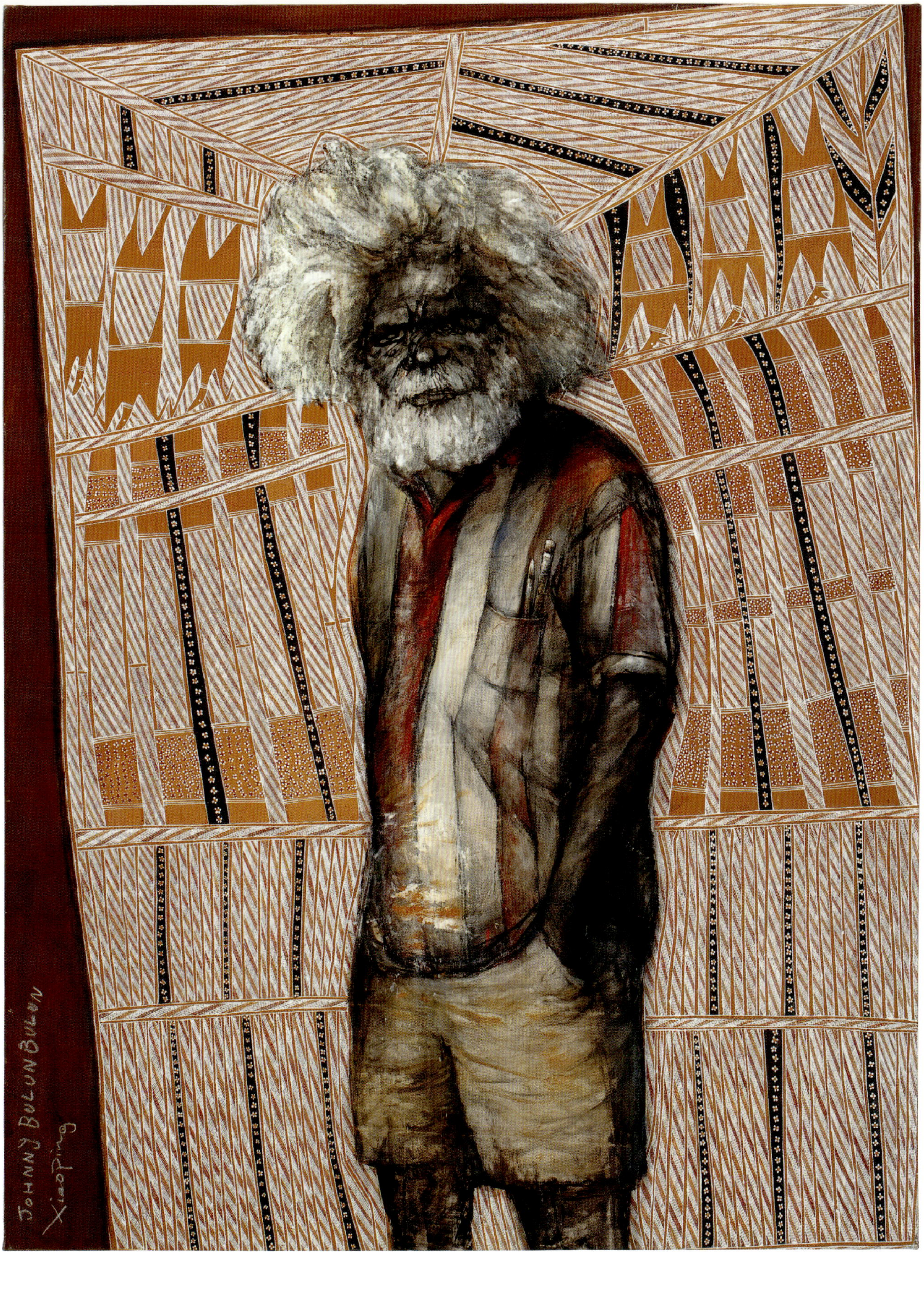
JOHNNY BULUNBULUN
Xiaoping

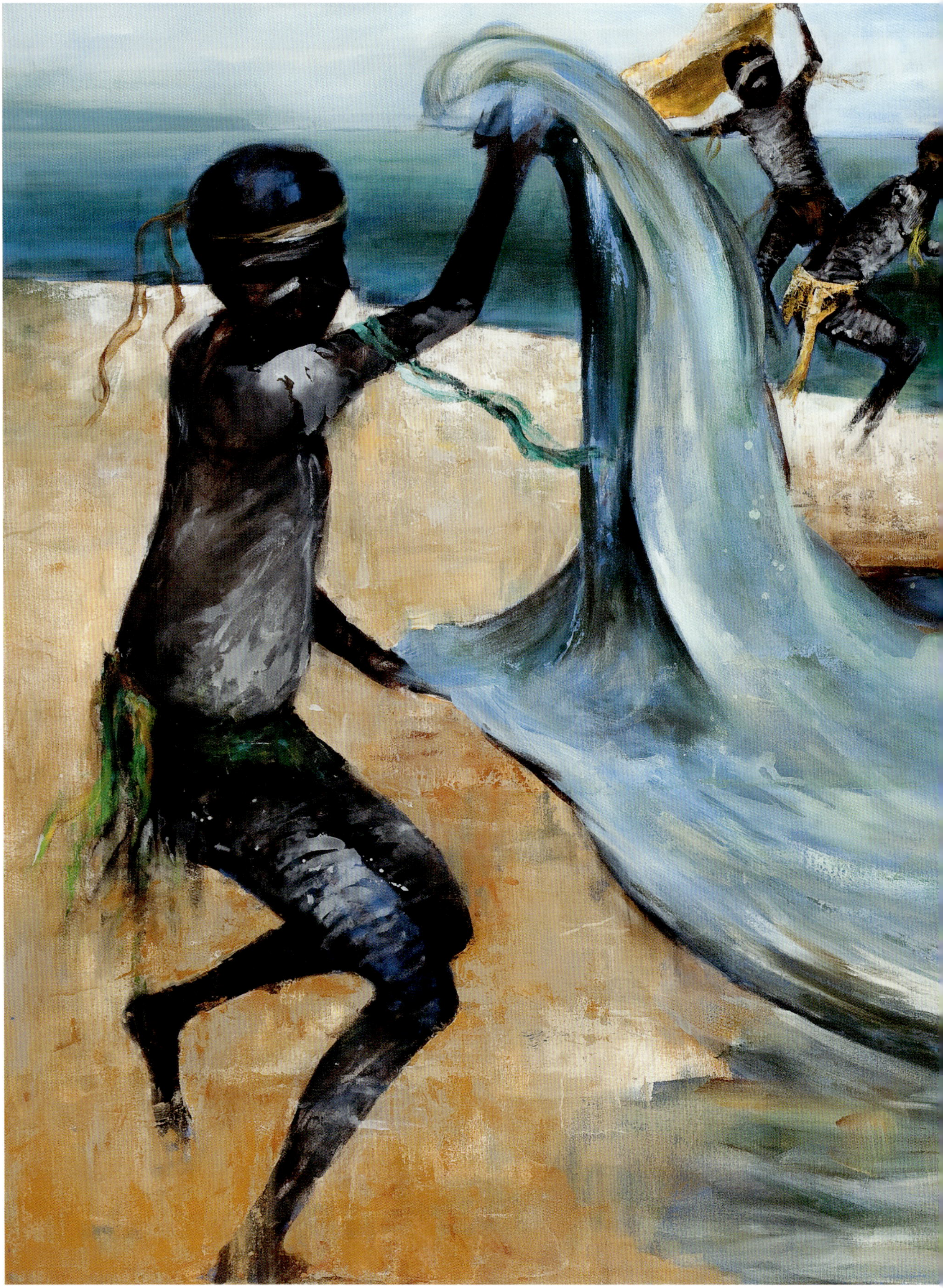

Zhou Xiaoping
The Source of Life
2010
Acrylic on canvas
165 x 230cm

周小平
生之源
2010年
丙烯，布面绘画
165 x 230cm

122

John Bulunbulun
& Zhou Xiaoping
Dialogue
2009
Acrylic and ochre
on canvas
240 x 170cm

约翰·布龙·布龙和周小平
对话
2009年
丙烯,天然色素,布面绘画
240 x 170cm

124

Zhou Xiaoping
Blue and White Bottle Vase with design from painting by John Bulunbulun
2010
Height: 37cm

周小平
青花天球瓶 —— 采用了约翰·布龙·布龙作品中的部分图案
2010年
高: 37cm

Zhou Xiaoping
Blue and White bowl with design from painting by John Bulunbulun (一)
2010
Diameter: 19cm

周小平
青花碗 —— 采用了约翰·布龙·布龙作品中的部分图案（一）
2010年
直径：19cm

127

128

Zhou Xiaoping
Blue and White bowl with design from painting by John Bulunbulun(二)
2010
Diameter: 19cm

周小平
青花碗 —— 采用了约翰·布龙·布龙作品中的部分图案(二)
2010年
直径: 19cm

John Bulunbulun
& Zhou Xiaoping
Discovery of trading
2009
Acrylic and ochre
on canvas
231.7 x 168.3cm

约翰·布龙·布龙和周小平
发现与交易
2009年
丙烯，天然色素，布面绘画
231.7 x 168.3cm

131

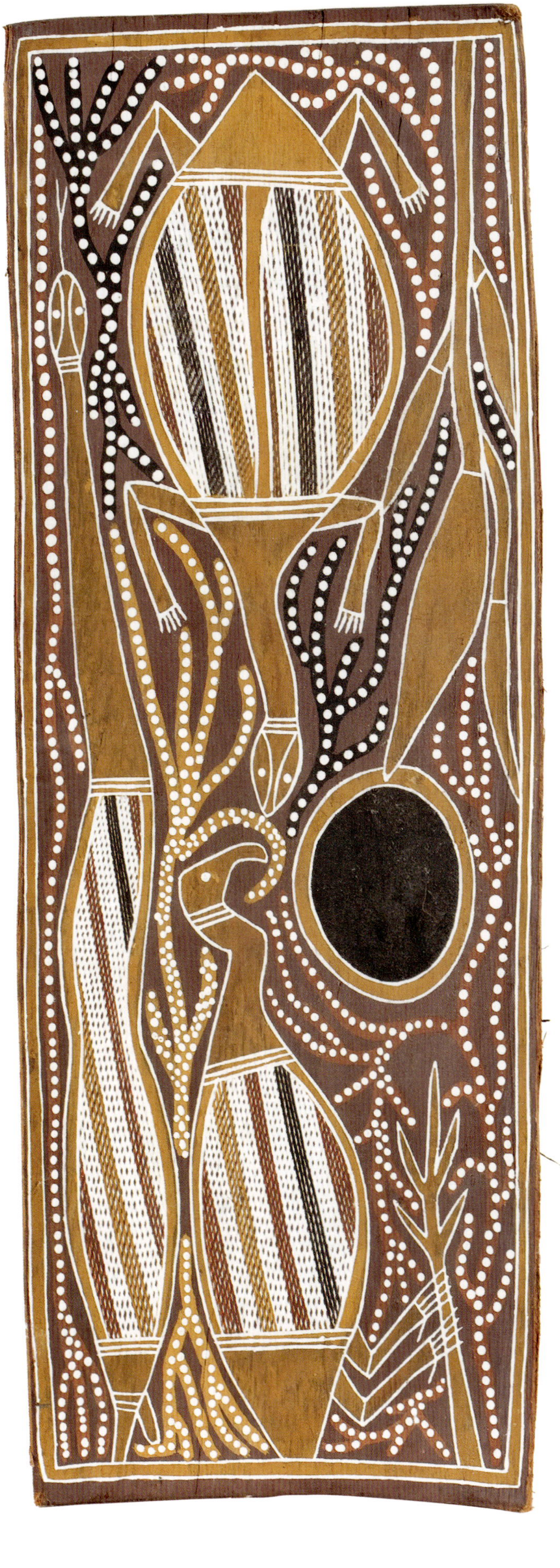

John Bulunbulun
Turtle
1991
Ochre pigments with PVC fixative on stringybark (Eucalyptus tetradonta)
83 x 28cm

约翰·布龙·布龙
龟 (布龙·布龙为小平所作的图腾树皮画)
1991年
树皮，PVC定色剂，天然色素
(四齿桉)
83 x 28cm

龟 ---- 是布龙·布龙为小平所作的图腾树皮画

1991年我和布龙·布龙，一位著名的澳洲土著画家，在 Maningrida 再次相遇。当时他正为如何在一张加工过的小树皮上画些什么陷入苦思。他使用了澳大利亞土著传统绘画(树皮画)所使用的特殊用料，那是由黄红两种石料，加上白色石膏粉和黑色木碳，所组成的四种颜料。

当他在石板上磨颜色时让我想起自己以前在中国书画所常用的墨塊和硯台。一种温暖熟悉的感觉瞬间又回到我的心中。我告诉布龙·布龙："让我为你磨颜色，你画画就行了。"

一连几天，我每天都去帮布龙·布龙磨颜色。那是一种由时间和耐心交织而成的艺术，每一个图案都是由許多线条组成，而那线条都是慢工细活一根一根画上去的。在这个过程中我深刻体会到土著画家的耐力与恆心。

阳光在林间闪爍，远处吹來的风总是夹杂丛林里的干热，我一边帮他磨颜色，一边听他介绍有关树皮画的作画过程和树皮画里的故事。

他是一个典型的丛林画家，他的绘画题材都是与土地和梦幻时代的故事有关。

而那些梦彷彿遙在天际，又近在眼前……有一天他突然对我说："Gojok（土著血緣里的一个名字），昨晚我做了一个梦，梦見了一只大海龟。"他指着面前树皮画上的一只龟说："就和这只一样。"

他专注而深情地看著自己的作品，表情严肅地说："在我们的文化里，每个人都会有一个属于自己的图腾。从现在起，龟就是你的图腾 。"

接著他用双手将画捧到我面前，郑重其事地说："它现在属于你的，Gojok, 我的兄弟。"沒有客套、沒有仪式，有的是人与人之间真挚流露的感情。

——周小平

"Turtle" – is the totem tree bark painting Bulunbulun created for Xiaoping

I met Bulunbulun, a famous Australian Aboriginal painter, again at Maningrida in 1991. At the time he was deep in thought about what to paint on the little piece of treated tree bark. He was working with the special materials used for traditional Australian Aboriginal painting (tree bark painting), which were the four types of pigments consisting of yellow and red mineral colours, as well as white gesso and black charcoal.

As he ground up the colours on the slab, it reminded me of the ink sticks and ink stones I frequently used in the past in Chinese calligraphy and painting. It inspired a sudden sense of warm familiarity in my memory. I told Bulunbulun: "Let me grind the colours for you, you can just paint."

For the next few days I went to help Bulunbulun grind colours every day, it is an art that combines both time and patience. Every picture is made of many lines, and those lines are slowly and finely painted on one by one. During this process I gained a deep understanding of the endurance and perseverance of Aboriginal painters.

The sunlight twinkles through the forest, and the winds that blow from afar are always blended with the dry heat of the bush. Whilst I grind the colours, I listen to him describe the tree bark painting process as well as the stories within the tree bark paintings.

He is a typical bush painter, the themes for his paintings come from the land and stories from the Dreamtime.

Those dreams seem to be over the horizon, yet they seem to be just before our eyes…. One day he suddenly said to me: "Gojok, (that is the Aboriginal skin name they gave me) last night I had a dream, I dreamt of a giant sea turtle," he pointed to a turtle on the tree bark painting in front of him: "Just like this one."

He stared intently and passionately at his own artwork, he solemnly said: "In our culture everyone has a totem that belongs to them, from now on, the turtle is your totem".

Next he presented the painting to me with both hands, he said seriously: "It now belongs to you, Gojok, my brother." There was no formality, no ceremony, what it did have was a revelation of the true feelings between two people.

Zhou Xiaoping

Zhou Xiaoping
Dissolve
2010
Scroll
215 x 73cm

周小平
交溶
2010年
卷轴
215 x 73cm

135

玛西亚·兰顿

澳大利亚国立大学文学士（优等生）、麦格理大学哲学博士、澳大利亚勋章获得者、澳大利亚社会科学院院士（作家、音景艺术家）。

玛西亚·兰顿目前就任墨尔本大学澳大利亚原住民研究学会首任主席，在此教书育人并开展原住民研究工作。她出版了很多著作，其中包括具有影响力的原住民电影、视频、艺术和艺术家主题作品，并多次获奖。她与Odette Mazel 及 Lisa Palmer 合作，在《澳大利亚人类学期刊》上发表了一篇关于望加锡人与雍古族人交往联系的文章。她为已故 Paddy Bedford、Brook Andrew、Destiny Deacon 等土著艺术家举办的展览所撰写目录文章，深受好评。作为一名学识卓越的人类学家与地理学家，她所发表的作品能够融汇贯通这些学科及历史领域。她曾在大型7集澳大利亚民族电视台（SBS）电视系列片《首批澳大利亚人》中担任高级顾问，并捉笔撰写了这部于2008年12月由墨尔本大学出版社出版的系列图书的主要章节。

MARCIA LANGTON
B.A. (Hons) ANU, PhD Macq. U., A.M., F.A.S.S.A. (Author, Soundscape Artist)

Marcia Langton holds the inaugural Chair of Australian Indigenous Studies at the University of Melbourne where she teaches and undertakes research on Indigenous people. She has published extensively, including seminal works on Aboriginal film, video, art and artists and has won awards for her writing. Along with Odette Mazel and Lisa Palmer, she has published an article on the Macassan involvement with Yolŋu people in *The Australian Journal of Anthropology*. Her catalogue essays for exhibitions by Aboriginal artists such as the late Paddy Bedford, Brook Andrew, Destiny Deacon, are highly regarded. Trained as anthropologist and geographer, her published work traverses these disciplines as well as history. She served as the Senior Consultant to the major 7- part SBS television series, *The First Australians*, and wrote substantial parts of the series book published by Melbourne University Press in December, 2008.

Marcia Langton
玛西亚·兰顿
Photo: Mark Ashkanasy
2010

约翰·布龙·布龙
艺术家
部落分支：Yirritja
部落：Gurrambakurramba

JOHN BULUNBULUN
Artist
Moiety: Yirritja
Clan: Gurrambakurramba

约翰·布龙·布龙不幸于2010年4月去世。备受尊重的土著艺术家约翰·布龙·布龙原在阿纳姆丛林Maningrida东部Wurdeja区，人们将其看作是阿纳姆丛林中部最重要的歌手之一。布龙·布龙多年来，荣获各类大奖，包括红赭石奖（2004年）、全国土著人和托雷斯海峡岛民艺术奖（2001年）品。澳大利亚多家大型美术馆收藏了他的作品。

It is with great sadness that John Bulunbulun passed away in April 2010. John Bulunbulun was a highly respected Aboriginal artist based in Wurdeja outstation, East of Maningrida, Arnhem Land. He was regarded as one of central Arnhem Land's most important song men. Bulunbulun won many awards and prizes over the years including the Red Ochre Award (2004) and the National Aboriginal and Torres Strait Islander Art Award (2001). His artwork has been collected by a number of Australia's major galleries.

John Bulunbulun
约翰·布龙·布龙

周小平
项目协调人、艺术家

ZHOU XIAOPING
Project Coordinator, Artist

周小平出生于中国，1988年他应邀赴澳大利亚举办个人画展，后定居墨尔本。自1988年，周小平曾先后多次深入澳洲北部的阿纳姆丛林和中西部荒漠上的金伯利（Kimberley）土著社区，与土著人共同生活和工作了三年之久。1992年，他受聘阿纳姆丛林曼宁格瑞达（Maningrida）土著社区学校，担任驻校艺术家。1996年，周小平在其中国合肥的故乡，和著名土著艺术家吉米·派克（Jimmy Pike）举办了他们的联合展览。这是第一个将澳大利亚土著文化艺术介绍到中国的展览。之后1999年他们又在北京的中国美术馆再次举办了他们的联展。自1988年赴澳大利亚以来，周小平在澳洲和世界各地共举办了34场个展，并出版了两本书。多年来，周小平多次获得澳洲政府设立的创作基金和写作基金。

Zhou Xiaoping was born in China and came to Australia in 1988 to exhibit his work in Melbourne. He has spent a total of three years living in the Aboriginal communities in Arnhem Land and in the Kimberley. In 1992 he was employed as the artist in residence at the Maningrida Community School in Arnhem Land. In 1996 Xiaoping and Aboriginal artist Jimmy Pike held a joint exhibition in Xiaoping's hometown, Hefei, China. This was the first time that Australia Aboriginal art featured in an exhibition in China. In 1999 Xiaoping and Pike held another joint exhibition at the National Gallery of China, Beijing. Since Xiaoping came to Australia in 1988 he has had 34 solo exhibitions and has also published two books.

Zhou Xiaoping
周小平
Photo: Mark Ashkanasy
2010

ACKNOWLEDGEMENTS

鸣谢

一流国际企业力拓(Rio Tinto)生产铝、铜、钻石、煤、铁矿、铀、金及工业矿物，参与金属与矿物生产中各个环节的工作。集团生产活动主要集中在澳大利亚和北美，业务遍及50多个国家，员工总数约达10.2万。

力拓十分尊重澳大利亚文化遗产所传承的重要意义，尤其是澳大利亚土著人的文化遗产；这些土著人是企业经营所在土地的传统监护人，与所在土地有着源远流长的历史渊源。中国市场是力拓业务的重要组成部分，集团也同样尊重中国文化传统所传承的历史意义及其所发挥的突出作用。

为了支持文化多样性，力拓非常荣幸能够赞助此次重要展览活动，纪念华人、望加锡人、澳大利亚土著人之间异乎寻常的贸易、协作以及永恒的友谊。

Rio Tinto is a leading international business involved in each stage of metal and mineral production. We produce aluminium, copper, diamonds, coal, iron ore, uranium, gold and industrial minerals. With production mainly from Australia and North America, the Group operates in more than 50 countries and employs about 102,000 people.

Rio Tinto respects the significance of Australia's cultural heritage, in particular that of Indigenous Australians who have traditional custodianship and historical connections to the land on which our businesses operate. China represents a significant part of Rio Tinto's business and the Group is equally respectful of the historical importance of Chinese culture and traditions and the prominent role they play.

In supporting cultural diversity, Rio Tinto is pleased to sponsor this important exhibition that celebrates the remarkable history of trade, collaboration and enduring relationships between Chinese, Macassan and Australian Aboriginal people.

RioTinto

THE UNIVERSITY OF MELBOURNE

首都博物馆
CAPITAL MUSEUM, CHINA

MUSEUM AND ART GALLERY NORTHERN TERRITORY | Northern Territory Government

GORDON DARLING FOUNDATION

Australia-China Council

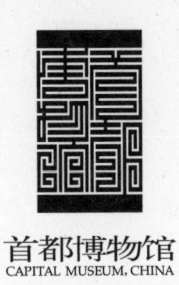

Australian Government
Department of Foreign Affairs and Trade

ACKNOWLEDGEMENTS

<u>Steering Committee</u>
Bruce Harvey
Jane Gronow
Daphne Morros
Elizabeth Marks
Marcia Langton
Sarah Morris
Robyn Sloggett
Suzanne Davies
Zhou Xiaoping
Dylan Brady
Robert Nudds
Stephanie Brady

Rio Tinto
Centre for Cultural Materials Conservation, University of Melbourne
Studio505
Studio Round
Reuben Fox
RMIT Gallery, RMIT University

The Steering Committee would like to acknowledge the vast personal commitment and effort of Professor Marcia Langton, without whose passion, determination and hard work over the last decade, this project would not have been possible.

<u>Artists</u>
Zhou Xiaoping
John Bulunbulun

<u>Curator and Exhibition Coordinator</u>
Sarah Morris

<u>Photography credits</u>
George Chaloupka: pp. 38
Mark Ashkanasy: Cover, endpaper, pp. 86–87 (colour image 2010), 90–91, 92, 94, 96–97, 98–99, 100–101, 102–103, 104–105, 106–107, 109, 110–111, 112–113, 114–115, 116–117, 119, 120–121, 122, 131, 132, 135, 137, 139.

Project acknowledgments

The participants and the steering committee would warmly like to thank the following: Anindilyakwa Art and Culture Centre; Anindilyakwa Land Council; Mark Ashkanasy; British Library; Chin Communications; Will Stubbs, Buku-Larrnggay Mulka Centre; 中国首都博物馆 —— 郭小凌 Guo Xiaoling, Director, 郝东晨 Hao Dongchen, 黄雪寅 Huang Xueyin, 鲁晓帆 Lu Xiaofan, 张靓 Zhang Liang, 包甦 Bao Su, 张杰 Zhang Jie, 赵妲 Zhao Da, 吕小晶 Lv Xiaojing of the Capital Museum, China; George Chaloupka; Emily Cheesman; Julian Cleary; Copyright holders; Aaron Corn; Lapulung Dhamarrandji and Stuart Porteous; Alejandra Duschatzky; Elcho Island Arts; The Hon Dr Craig Emerson Australian Minister for Trade; Fiona Finlayson; Djangirrawuy Garawirrtja; Gordon Darling Foundation; Dr Joseph Gumbula; Charlotte Harris Rees, Dr Hendon M. Harris Jr Map Collection; Hong Kong University of Science and Technology; Alison Inglis; International Art Services; Laurie Ma-Arbudug and Paul Pascoe; Anna Malgorzewicz; Deborah Reich and Claire Summers, Maningrida Arts and Culture; Paul Clarke, Christine Tarbett-Buckley, Sue Bassett, Sandra Yee, Ilka Schacht, Museum and Art Gallery of the Northern Territory; Lindy Allen, Elizabeth McCartney, Melanie Raberts, Rosemary Wrench, Museum Victoria; Alan Marett; Odette Mazel; National Archives of Australia; National Gallery of Australia; National Library of Australia; James Bradley and Rachel Clements, Nirvana Films Pty Ltd; Northern Territory Library; Lisa Palmer; POD Museum and Art Services; Julia Postle; Jelmer Procee; Dr Geoff Raby, Australian Ambassador to China; Jill Collins, Amanda Barry, Zhang Hong, Katie Tian and Xin Li Australian Embassy, Beijing; Elizabeth Marks, Mark O'Neill, Kimberley Sceresini, Tony Shaffer, Rio Tinto; Associate Professor Robyn Sloggett and Tim Ould, Centre for Cultural Materials Conservation, University of Melbourne; Tim Smith; Kartia Snoek; State Library of New South Wales; State Library of South Australia; Mrs Dortia Thomson and the Donald Thomson Collection; Jane Ulman; University of Melbourne; Julia Mant, University of Sydney Archives; John Stanton and Barbara Matters, University of Western Australia Berndt Museum of Anthropology; Djalalingba Yunupingu; Galarrwuy Yunupingu; Mandawuy Yunupingu; Zhou Xiaoping & family.

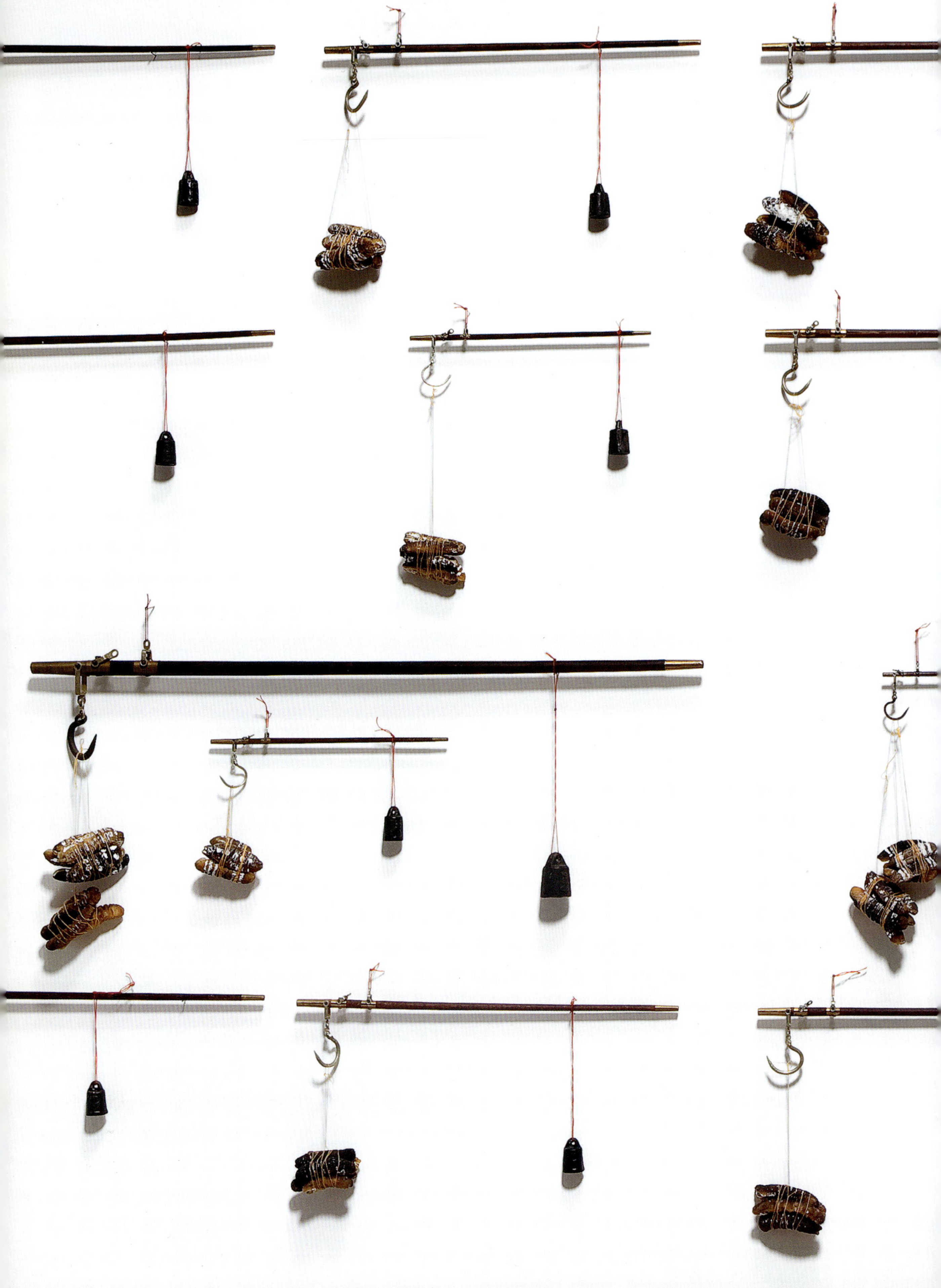